HEALING MY WOUNDS

Mª Teresa Fageus

Independently published

Title: HEALING MY WOUNDS

Maria Teresa Fageus © 2024

Cover: Isabel Jimenez

Layout: Sandra García @correccionessandrag

Traslation: Emil Fageus

I hope my story helps people in their spiritual growth.
The change starts with you. You are the example you want to see in the world.
You can't convince anyone because we are not in their thoughts.

THANKFULNESS

My name is Maria Teresa, I have sixty-six years old. I am a single mother with two wonderful children.

The oldest of them, Jonathan, was born with cerebral palsy, he is currently thirty years old; the second of my children, Emil; He is twenty-six years old, a very spiritual person and one hundred percent athlete. Currently live in Sweden, a Nordic country, where tranquility and equality reign, something that I really like because of my personality.

I was born in Peru, I had wonderful parents. I honour them by telling my story. I know that they accompany me from a plane higher than the earth, where everything is peace and spirituality.

I am very happy that they have returned home, where our origin is from, for being spiritual beings, living a human experience, here on this planet Earth, which is a great school of souls, and we choose the exams that we have to pass here before being born, for the evolution of our awareness.

This is my story that my soul chose before I was born, together with all the souls that collaborated, in an act of unconditional love, for my learning and spiritual growth.

I am the fourth of ten brothers, I had a very hard childhood, my father was violent, I received physical punishments. This greatly influenced my personality since childhood wounds have a high emotional impact.

I know that my parents did everything the best they could, with the tools they had at that time.

My parents were financially poor, but despite that, we never lacked anything. Neither clothes nor food. My dad worked very hard to support his ten children, who were two years apart.

My mom was a great woman, so brave and hardworking that she took care of all of us. She always kept us very clean and cared for, she cooked delicious.

Many times, I remember the dishes she prepared.

My dad didn't cook much, but when he did, he seemed like a great chef.

He was a good example of a father for all of us, at least for me, he was my friend, I trusted him a lot, I never saw him drunk, nor with infidelities with my mother, at least, that's what I perceived as a child.

I assume that the violence my father had was due to the stress of so much responsibility with us and with my mother, so that nothing bad would happen to us.

My mother, on one occasion, told me about my father's childhood.

It was really very, very hard for a child, I felt sad and moved by him, by what he had experienced. There I realized that despite the physical punishments he gave us, he gave us everything that he couldn't have, and I value that very much.

I realized since I was a child and even more so, when I became a mother and did the same thing, I gave my children everything that I didn't have, like my parents did. That is why I invite all children, before judging their parents, to find out what their childhood was like.

Even though when you are a child, you interpret very dramatic and hard events, which really are for an innocent child, who does not understand why, however, when we are adults, we have to take charge of healing our childhood wounds., so as not to get trapped in those traumas.

Our own parents have carried their own traumas from their childhood, which they have not been able to transcend.

We have come to this world to heal our wounds and transcend them, which is the reason for our suffering with spiritual knowledge.

We are spiritual souls, living a human experience, we make a pact before being born with other souls, in an act of unconditional love, to learn the lessons that life gives us and transcend them so that they are not repeated over and over throughout this material world. in which we live.

When I was a child, I always thought that, when I grew up and could, I would reward my dad for all the sacrifice he made for all of us. I never thought about the blows. Just to thank him for his effort.

PREDICTIONS OF THE FUTURE

My mother told me, when I was older, that when I was seven years old, one time, we were all eating together at the table, I got up and told everyone that I was going to travel around the world, I was going to speak a lot of languages and was going to earn a lot of money. Then I sat down and continued eating. I don't remember anything about this episode, but that's how it was in the future. Now I live in Sweden and speak seven languages.

I remember at school that I sold my avocado bread and cakes at recess time, so I could pay for my school supplies, save money and not bother my dad. I wanted to be rich.

At the age of twelve, I already had a bank account at the bank.

On one occasion, my dad taught me how to make some tofes of chocolate and I found it very interesting. I started making them to sell at school, so much so that I became obsessed with sales and my parents no longer let me use the kitchen to prepare my toffees and I went to a school friend's house. Her mother understood me and made her cooking easier for me.

For my parents, I was very ambitious and that was wrong, according to their perspectives, I only had one goal: TO BE RICH.

However, I always realized that he took me to the best schools, and I was, in some way, his favourite daughter... We could say that I was very intelligent. The courses that I liked the most were Spanish grammar, shorthand, English, mathematics and accounting.

At the age of sixteen, already in high school, I had a friend, I still remember her, who when classes finished, we would walk around residential places. I loved seeing wonderful houses, big mansions. I really enjoyed it, and we asked ourselves:

—Which one do you like more?

To which I responded:

—I like that one, and that's how I want to have it!

I said it with great enthusiasm... And, luckily, that was the case in the future, I like having houses. It's my passion.

THE LAW OF ATTRACTION

The place where we lived was poor, however, I dressed very elegantly, with the money I saved from my sales; And I had a very distinguished walk, it was natural for me, not because I felt superior to my entire neighbourhood, but because I felt that was my identity.

In fact, I had very few friends in my neighbourhood, only other people from another social level.

And all that way of being, now that I read books on the law of attraction, are behaviours of autosuggestion, which says,

«FEEL LIKE YOU ALREADY ARE».

However, I applied the laws of the universe in a natural way, without having studied them. I am sure that I came with this well-developed knowledge from past lives.

The universe is mental, and everything is energy and vibration. If a person is vibrating at the height of his dreams, thinking that he already has it... That wish comes true. I know we all have that ability from birth, but we have to change our beliefs and paradigms. We are not destined; we are programmed by the whole system of beliefs.

SYNCHRONICITIES OF THE UNIVERSE

In the universe, God, the higher self, or whatever you want to call it, rules the same thing: cause and effect. In order to see your dreams come true, you have to give, because a dream without action is an illusion.

There are no miracles.

When you visualize with a firm assurance that your dream is already a fact and give thanks in advance, believing that you already have it, and do your part on the way to that dream, the universe confabulates and helps you find the means to achieve it, this is called synchronicities.

You do everything, everything, everything that is in your hands, and the Universe lavs everything at your feet.

Because of my performance in the English course, I was awarded two scholarships to study the language, after I finished high school.

Study American English and British English.

Subsequently, I met the director of the Alliance Française.

A French man very nice, I always remember him.

Roger was his name, he gave me a scholarship to study French. I studied French for free at a very expensive academy. Always thanking God, universe, for so many blessings.

On one occasion, leaving my English academy, I met an Austrian, I liked to be able to practice English, he also spoke a little Spanish, but I told him that we should speak both languages, so that I could practice it, since I was studying.

We became friends, he was a tourist in Peru, and later he was my crush. I introduced him to my family, and he was very well received by my parents and my brothers, he was a very simple and empathetic person.

He was traveling to Austria and returned to visit me. I did a lot of adventure trips with him, I loved them, like every young person.

On one of the times he came to Peru, we took a trip through Peru, Colombia and Bolivia, all by train. We were in the Amazon, with the natives, visiting their huts, learning more about their Indian culture. It was very nice.

We did a tour package with a group of foreigners, and we lived in a bungalow, very rustic, near the river, with the sounds of fish, birds and animals, all wonderful.

One afternoon, everyone agreed to jump in the Amazon and swim, there were a lot of mosquitoes, I didn't know how to swim.

My boyfriend gave me a life jacket, he told me I wasn't going to sink, I was so panicked that I hesitated to jump in.

The whole group, which was already in the water, was looking at me waiting for me to jump in, but I couldn't, the mosquitoes were biting me and finally I didn't jump in, I didn't have the courage. My lover, with a flushed face, said to me:

«Shame on you, don't even jump with your life jacket».

Well, it was an experience, but the next day, ironically very early in the morning, I walked to the same place, I wanted to wash my shoes in the river, it was a port that had wood covered in mud, but there was nowhere to hold on.

Everything was quiet, as the guests were having breakfast at the hotel restaurant, including my boyfriend.

As I approached the dark water, I took off my shoes and prepared to sit down to wash them.

I began to slip through the mud of the wood with my shoes in my hands and having nowhere to hold on. Little by little while I slipped, I couldn't help but fall, there was no one there, everything was still completely silent, and I started to get scared.

I kept looking at the waters, which were dark green, almost black.

I fell, I went up and down, I didn't know how to swim, I thought it was the end, that I was going to drown, and worst of all, my boyfriend and all the other people were very calm, having breakfast, while I was foolishly drowning.

On a head climb, I saw a dwarf. I always remember his physical appearance, very small, with the face larger in proportion to the body, he shook my hand and pulled me out of the water in one go.

What a great force, I think now, I was so scared.

«Thank you», | said as I left.

shook off my clothes and when I looked up, I was gone. I looked sideways, I didn't understand anything; And I went back to where they were all having breakfast. They looked at me in amazement, I arrived all wet, I told them that I had fallen, and a little dwarf saved my life. I asked the bungalow guides who it was, and no one knew. I went back to the site, and I didn't see him, I never saw him again. What I did think from that moment of the event until now, after almost forty years, was that, how could such a small person have so much strength to be able to pull me out with just one hand. It was truly an otherworldly force, because if not, it has no other explanation. It was a miracle from God!

After a week, our trip continued on the train that was going from Peru to Colombia, a very long trip, it broke down and in order to have a new connection, we had to get off at a station where there was no one, it looked like a desert, full of sand. The other passengers on the train continued walking in another direction. We stayed in a booth to wait for the next connection that would arrive in five hours, that's what the timetable sign said. | remember it was very hot. My boyfriend told me that I sat on the sand and stared at a spot and stayed in that meditative state for five hours.

He told me about this event two years later, because I don't remember anything, it's as if he hadn't lived that moment.

After that, we travelled to Bogota, we went to make a visit with a tour group to the Montserrat mountain, is very famous in Colombia. After the excursion with the group, we went alone and preferred to walk a little around, there was a street that was downhill, it looked very quiet, the houses were in good condition, but yes, you could not see people, as I did not know that country, as much as mine, I thought it was all normal.

My boyfriend always had his camera tied around his waist with a chain, he was a fan of photos, he had many memories, when we met after thirty years, he still kept all the photos of our travels.

Well, we kept walking, at that point I saw two men coming in the opposite direction of us, but I noticed that they were very indiscreet, because they were looking directly at the waist of the two of us, I think to see if we had weapons. They passed us without taking their eyes off us. That gave me a very big suspicion and I said to my boyfriend:

«Why do they look at us so strangely?».

I told him we had to be careful.

We started walking faster, until we started running, they immediately put their hands under their jackets and started yelling at us:

—¡Stop, stop!

They must have thought we didn't speak Spanish. They took their hands out of their shirts... And what I could see!

They had tremendous knives as big as an axe, I remember they were very big and sharp, they were made like tin, very sharp knives.

The only thing I did when I saw them coming towards us was to put my hands to my stomach, because I thought they were going to put that knife in me, and I said to them:

—No, no.

They came up to us, one to me and the other to my lover.

They reached almost a little more than the Austrian's waist, they looked very small, typical Colombians, who are not so tall.

On the other hand, the Austrian was over eight meters tall and quite corpulent, he used to carry a very small Swiss knife, since it had the Swiss flag, something very typical because they use it for different needs. It was more domestic than to defend himself, but the Austrian took out a small knife and confronted him, told him to give him the briefcase and he said no. The Colombian threw slashes so that it reached his neck, but he dodged them by shaking his head and threatened him with his knife, which looked like a toy next to the axes they had.

On the other hand, the Colombian grabbed me by the neck with one hand and with the other he grabbed the knife threatening me.

«Tell him to hand over the suitcase! ». He yelled at me.

Asked him please, but he kept refusing to.

At one point I realized that the Colombian who had me by the neck was very distracted looking at the Austrian, so I took advantage of it, and in a life-or-death instant, | elbowed him and ran away very terrified in the direction of the car track.

It was about fifty meters from where the two Colombians were with the Austrian at that moment.

I was screaming on the car track, while I was looking at what was happening with my boyfriend, I was desperate, it was a nightmare.

The first car passed, I stood in the middle of the track with my arms up making emergency stops and if I didn't get out of the way, they would have run over me, they didn't stop.

Continued, calling for help on the tarmac, very scared and worried about my boyfriend. I could see him in the distance fighting, with the two of them.

Until a second car came, this one did stop, it was a taxi, with many people inside, it was going to collective transport, they opened the door and said:

Come up, quick.

Then I yelled at my boyfriend:

—Come, run, come!

The criminals got scared and ran away. They just yelled at me:

«Damn! ». But they had so much hatred in their eyes that if they had had me around, they would have stung me to pieces.

We got into the taxi trembling, they gave Harald paper to dry the blood, because one of the knives had reached his neck very slightly.

We were calmed down by the people in the taxi because I was stuttering, I had never experienced something so frightening up close. We thanked them, they had saved our lives.

When we arrived at the hotel, we hugged, I was in shock, very scared, we got ready and decided to tell some policemen who were near the hotel. We told him that this happened near the hill of Monserrat.

Although they told us that we were privileged to be alive, that it was the most dangerous place in Bogota and that the police do not enter there because there is a lot of risk of not getting out alive.

couldn't believe my ears. Once again, God saved us.

For a year, my boyfriend would come and go from Austria to Peru to visit me, until when I was twenty-one, he proposed that I go to Austria to meet and later marry him.

Well, I accepted and so did my parents, they had a lot of confidence in me.

I thought about taking my older sister with me so that she could have a better future and thank God, my parents agreed.

In Austria, I felt very well, everything was so different, so clean, the landscapes were very beautiful, although very cold in the winter. It was in Salzburg that I saw, for the first time, hailstones of snow falling.

I was in a coffee shop with him, and it was really fantastic, to see something like that.

However, I didn't adapt, I wanted to study German, which I didn't talk about at home with my boyfriend. He went to work very early every day, I was alone with my sister, we went out during the day to visit Vienna and get to know, but on weekends, the three of us went out, to museums, parks, etc.

I really liked the world of modelling, earning much money and help my parents and my brothers. I thought about them every day. I know that he did everything possible for me to agree to marry him and have children, a family, but I was not ready to be a mother so early, I wanted to see the world, to see beyond...

Once, when I was going out with my sister, I met a very beautiful brunette from Haiti, she told me that she worked as a model in Switzerland.

She told me about Switzerland, which was a very rich country and which, in the modelling environment, was very advanced internationally, as it had borders with France, Italy and Germany. In particular, he mentioned Paris, a city that had a lot of potential in the world of fashion.

I was very enthusiastic about everything she told me, I talked to my boyfriend, of course he didn't like the idea of me going to another country, but at that time I was young, very determined and I had to do what I liked, not conform.

Finally, he had to accept, it was my life.

We never lost touch and I always visited him, while was in Switzerland.

We travelled to Switzerland, Zurich, more specifically.

There I learned Italian, French and German, so I speak all three languages.

I found a modelling academy, I was delighted! How I liked it!

In spite of all my classmates at the academy, they were very tall, I had a lot of confidence to walk on catwalks, the teacher told them:

Look at Maria Theresa how she walks.

She always showed me as a sample.

I got my mannequin certificate and worked as a runway model and also a photo model.

I was also in the world of sales, I discovered that gold and jewellery were what people wore the most, they dressed very elegantly.

From there came an idea in me, to sell gold jewellery with Inca designs, I bought it in Peru and sold it in the boutiques that were located on a main street in Zurich, the most expensive in the world.

I had my clients, I offered them my jewellery, and I managed to sell it for ten times more than what I bought in Peru.

Actually, started to earn a lot of money, I was doing what I liked which was modelling and also sales, which I did in Peru at a very young age.

My driving force was always to help my family, without that desire, I don't think I would have been able to earn so much.

Here, I emphasize what my mom told me on the trips I made to Peru when I visited them. That I, at the age of seven, told them that I was going to speak many languages, I was going to know many countries and I was going to have a lot of money.

She told me about it herself, when I was twenty-five years old, because what I said as a child was happening. I don't remember that part as a child, it was erased from my mind.

After two years of living in Switzerland, I sent a ticket for my sister, who was two years older than me. She had her little boy, was a single mother and I wasn't having a very good time in Peru.

She came to Switzerland, I was very happy, we were already three sisters, and very soon after living in Switzerland, I introduced her to a French Swiss, they met, fell in love, and got married. They had three daughters.

Later, he travelled to Peru to meet my sister's family and son, who was seven years old at the time and had stayed with our parents.

The boy was very naughty, I always remember his mischief.

Their little son travelled with them and stayed to live in Switzerland for the rest of his life, now a young man of forty-eight, with three wonderful children, a girl and two boys.

And so, I invited all my brothers and sisters to Switzerland, except for two of them. The eldest, who was already independent from a very early age, currently lives in Brazil and, of course, my parents, who travelled several times, and stayed for long periods living in that beautiful country.

The sixth of my brothers didn't travel either, the reason, I don't remember exactly, but he certainly didn't want to travel.

All the others have travelled to Switzerland many times, but unfortunately, they did not take advantage of the opportunity and did not stay to settle. They currently live in Peru, except my younger sister, who lives in Chile.

My older sister, who initially travelled with me to Austria, met a Swiss man, very kind, simple, spoke perfect Spanish, had previously lived in Spain, they had two wonderful children, a boy and a little woman who are now very handsome young men.

A few years later, in Switzerland, I met a man in the modelling environment, he was also a model.

When I saw him the first time, I had a feeling that he was a relative, a first cousin or something, I can't explain it, but he didn't have the colour of my skin, he was white.

We got along well, in short, we lived eight years together.

However, they were not the best years of my life. The first year of meeting him, I realized that he was an alcoholic, I got into a lot of trouble for defending him, as he was very aggressive with people when he drank alcohol.

But I don't know why I couldn't get out of that relationship, it was something like a dependency that I had, I always told myself that he was going to change, and he never did and so the eight years went by, full of ups and downs.

Once, among all the lies he told me, he convinced me to have a joint bank account, I, for reasons of life, accepted, decided to trust.

A year later, after seeing his behaviour getting worse and worse, I decided to go check my account at the bank and I was surprised, because I had nothing. I felt immense sadness and disappointment, not because of the money itself, but because of the deception. I realized that I was a very innocent person.

I had left my parents' house to face the jungle, where there were people with feelings that I did not know.

Envy, in the environment where I worked, was very common, there were too many people who cheated like that, and I couldn't understand it, I didn't know that there were people like that.

I had to start again from scratch, and I was able to recover quickly with my work.

During that time and together with my sister, we help my dad build the house financially.

The rest of my brothers also helped, as they worked in the construction that my dad directed, since his profession was an engineer.

My parents` house was finished in six months. Very nice, my parents were very happy, we left the old house in the poor neighbourhood and now they lived in their dreams house.

It was very rewarding to see that whole process.

When I visited them, we went out to eat almost every day and went to events with the whole family, we had a great time moment.

The three sisters used to travel all the time when we were still single.

They were unforgettable moments, I saw my parents laughing, without any concern for money, everything was perfect like a fairy dream.

However, with the experience of my partner's betrayal, I entered a state of sadness because of so much disappointment, although mysteriously, | became very spiritual, I began to be interested in the behaviour of the human being.

I wondered over and over again where the envy came from, since in the modelling world it was the order of the day.

It didn't fit in me, I didn't envy anyone, I knew that each person shone with their own light and never compared me, on the contrary, I admired when I saw a talented person.

In Switzerland, I started collecting some small books that......

They were called Selections, I liked it, because there were philosophical phrases that appealed to me a lot, phrases, and parables from the bible.

I started to save them; I didn't know why.

A short time later, the desire to speak to dangerous prisoners in prisons was born in me, since I was twenty-seven years old, I think it was a call from my soul, I was interested in that type of personality, because I knew that they had stayed in some childhood trauma, which made them change their good side, its essence or perhaps some bad experience as an adult.

I wanted to tell them about my experience and so I did, after fifteen years and which I will tell you later; Desire always remained alive in my heart.

Living with this couple, over the course of the eight years, we once travelled by car from Switzerland to Denmark. On the way we briefly passed through Sweden, a country totally unknown to me at that time.

We parked at a tap, where there was a shop with typical Swedish objects and ornaments. It caught my attention, a baby clothes. I noticed clearly that it was for men, made of ceramic, dark beige almost brown, there were three pieces: the top part was the baby's shirt, the bottom part was a paal breeches and some shoes, all in ceramic and had very small, the label of the Swedish flag, I realized this detail a few years later.

I bought the pottery and brought it to Switzerland, I put it as decoration on the wall of a spiritual room in my apartment, which I used for meditation.

After a year, I bought a house in Spain on the Coast Golden.

An hour from Barcelona, specifically in Tarragona, which was in the middle of construction, and I had the opportunity to make some changes if I wished.

The house had three floors, basement, entrance floor and second floor. I directed them to the architects and told them that, instead of using the basement, as they use in Spain to store their wines. I wanted to make rooms for my guests, and I wanted a lot of small windows, they laughed because in Spain, they were not used to that type of house. They even called it the house of a thousand windows.

I didn't know at the time, that I was building a typical Swedish house with many windows in the basement, which they used to use for laundry and storage of the things in each apartment.

After a few years, when I got to know Sweden, I saw it and I was amazed.

When the construction was finished, I bought furniture, some I bought in Switzerland and brought to Spain, among other things, I took the nifo ceramics that I had bought in Sweden, I treated it with a lot of care, apart from the fact that the material was very delicate.

In one of the basement bedrooms, I put the decorative ceramics on the wall and decorated it with wooden beds. All very rustic.

The other room, I decorated it more European, with very modern beds, and very modern paintings.

PREMOTIONS DREAMS

During my time in Switzerland, at the age of twenty-five, I was diagnosed with an orange-sized fibroid on my ovaries, after having so much muscle pain during my menstrual periods, which caused anaemia.

One night I dream i was passing by the house of my nephew Roger, who was very small and I asked him if he wanted to accompany me on my trip, it was clear in the dream, that I was sad and I was saying goodbye, he told me no, I continued to look for my little sister, the youngest, she would have been seven years old at the time, I asked her the same question and she said no and I continued to be very sad; I loved them very much, they were like my children, my sister was born when I was fifteen years old.

Then another week passed, the day of the operation was approaching and a few days before I had a dream, which was like a nightmare.

And when I woke up, I was very distraught.

I dreamed that I was in a village, but there were no inhabitants, only a group of people who wanted to kill me, I ran and ran to escape, I crossed the tracks, crossed the streets and saw a taxi, I stopped it and the driver took me to another group of people who wanted to end my life, miraculously I escaped from that group of people who were hooded. I climbed a building, climbed the stairs to the top and on the roof, I found another group of people who took me to a Lord with a white beard, he was sitting. I thought I couldn't get away anymore, I was tired, and I thought it was the end, I gave up, but the Lord said to me in a serious and firm voice, very serene:

This time, he is going to forgive me, but I had to go to a country where no one knows me.

It was the Master Jesus of Nazareth. After many years understood the message, it was the country of Sweden, where I live today.

I assumed he was referring to Switzerland, it was a very rich country, but there was also a lot of freedom. In the modelling world, there was a lot of envy and competition, you could easily lose a model to drugs, alcohol, etc.

The day of the operation arrived, I was in a hospital room sharing with three other people, we all made beautiful friends, the next day they took me to have surgery, everything went well, but when they returned me to the room after surgery, they left me a device with cords that were in my heart, it was like an electrocardiogram and it stayed with me. They all asked me why I had that device, I told them I didn't know. Then in the afternoon my friends came to visit me, they brought me fruits. I really felt fantastic, I sat down, and it looked like I hadn't had surgery, I thought it was going to come out next time day.

That same day, in the night, already sleeping, I woke up jumping out of bed, with all the cables I had, the device that had been left to me was to revive my heart when it stopped; It seems that the doctors knew I was going to have a cardiac arrest, but they didn't tell me anything, so as not to scare me.

The alarm sounded, many doctors and nurses arrived, I kept jumping and my chest burned like fire, then they stabilized me, but I was left with that pain in my chest for a few more days, especially when I went to sleep, which felt like anguish. I was always under observation.

There I understood that God, in that dream, told me that He was going to save my life on that occasion.

I also had a dream that repeated itself many times and I always woke up crying very sadly. I used to dream my mom would tell me what I had helped them and my whole family with, that made me very sad because I always helped them in those moments. But this happened after a few years, just as I had dreamed.

During my years in Switzerland, I realized that I had a trauma with my mom and always, when I had a drink with my friends, I talked to them about the same thing, when my mom punished me by leaving me without food for a month, when I answered her badly and that hurt me a lot until I was almost thirty-five years old. After I had my first child, that trauma disappeared. curiously.

LAW OF KARMA AND PAST LIVES

One night, while I was sleeping, I had a regression to past lives, I heard a voice that told me- I remember it like it was yesterday; to hold my breath and I came out of a belly button and the umbilical cord was holding me up and I was falling headlong down, I felt an emptiness in my stomach because of the way I was falling at full speed and when I got there I saw myself up, myself.

It was a farm, the floor was dirt, there was little light, it seems that there were only lamps. I was looking at a man, he was like a foreman on a farm, he had his slaves, and he was holding a newborn child in his hands. !!That foreman was me!! My mother was in front of me on her knees, she was my slave, who asked me for mercy crying to give her11 son and I told her screaming that No!!

It made me very sad to see my mom like that from above.

I understood that this was in past lives. My mom was my slave who had a child with me. I took that child from her and he was the man I knew in this life, who took all my money from the bank in Switzerland.

They made me see what was the reason that I was living, that karma with my mom and that I was paying for it in this existence.

Then I woke up, but at the time, I wasn't so aware because I didn't think much of it until the last few years.

However, I realized, in this life, that my mom had a lot of affection for that man, when I visited her in Peru, it was something very special, she laughed a lot with him. I saw her very happy.

Over time, I understood what my partner's role was, he was her son in another life.

SYNCHRONICITIES OF MY DESTINY

Then I started traveling to many countries with my partner, but I also travelled alone to Haiti, Cuba and Brazil. On one occasion, when I was alone in Cuba, in my hotel, I wanted to take a nap and I dreamed that a Cuban who was thin, typical Cuban, told me that I was going to meet my partner at an airport at seven o'clock at night.

I remember that I used to go to Zurich airport many times at that time to see if I would meet the love of my life, since I had already ended that previous relationship.

I was very excited at the airport until I got tired, and I said to myself: «I'm not going to think about that anymore and that's it».

So it happened, I think eight months later and... I once travelled to Peru alone and asked my family if they wanted to travel with me to Mexico.

They didn't want to get to know the country.

I asked my younger sister if she wanted to visit Cancun, to come with me, and my mom told me:

«Why don't you travel alone? ». Enjoy life! You always want to take someone!

And finally, so I did, I went to Cancun alone, to that country I didn't know.

MY TRIP TO CANCÚN

The day of my trip arrived, I did it alone, a little nervous and shy, because I knew that Cancun was a romantic place, where most people went as a couple. Of course, I planned my trip, I booked a hotel in Peru, in a beautiful area in Cancun, I saw it through a travel agency, when I got there, I was very disappointed, because the place was not as beautiful or new as the photos. So, I spent the first night, then decided to look for a good hotel with all its amenities myself.

I found a beautiful one, very good attention from the hotel staff, I looked for tourist agencies to know typical sites on the site, it was really a very nice trip. I met a lot of new people in the tour group I was going to, I had my tour guide to myself.

He came to pick me up from the hotel, to take me to some islands.

A journey full of adventures. I stayed in Cancun for ten days.

I went to the nightclubs, Virgin Islands and typical food places of the country, with mariachis singing in the restaurants.

Then I wanted to travel to Acapulco, it's a very traditional place, I thought, I should know it! On my trip to Acapulco, I had to pass through transit at the airport in Mexico, which is the capital. A very large airport, I had to wait an hour to continue to Acapulco, my final destination.

I was very distracted and suddenly I saw almost two hundred meters away a tall, elegant, blond man. He was tall, but I saw him as a giant in the midst of the people and a golden light shining on his sides.

All the people who were close to him came up to his waist.

When I saw him, I said to myself, I would like to marry this man. It was love at first sight, it seemed that only he existed.

At the same time, I knew he was a manager, and he was upset that his employees had done a bad job, he confirmed this to me, when we spoke later. I'll tell you about it later.

I was so shocked that I stood still and immediately reacted, because I felt shyness and embarrassment for having stared for so long.

He, in turn, when he saw me, dropped some folders that he was carrying to look at me, even though we were far away from each other. He had to pick up his things from the floor. He carried a light-leather briefcase in his hand. He knew my emotional state, how I felt at the time, he told me later.

Incredible!

I smiled and turned to go on my way, crestfallen... I kept walking, I passed a long corridor, I had to go to a room, I don't remember the number, but the airport was huge, I lost sight of that man, I forgot, looking for my waiting room.

I arrived at the room bound for Acapulco, I sat down to wait and a little more than fifteen minutes passed, and what was my surprise that this man entered the same room.

—Wuauuu! I said to myself.

I felt shy, but I was also hugely attracted to it. He saw me, his look very elegant, he looked at me and sat down the continuous seat in front of me, he looked at my shoes, I know he wanted to talk to me, but I think he got shy, and I started talking to him, I couldn't wait, I asked him if he had a cigarette, to start the conversation.

My way of being wasn't like that, I had never started a conversation with a man, on the contrary, they always spoke to me first, but with him I couldn't wait, I don't know what was really wrong with me, something I couldn't control.

He said yes and gave me a cigarette. He asked my name, and I asked his.

He asked me where I was from, I told him from Peru, but that I lived in Switzerland. He told me he was Swedish, but he worked in

Acapulco. That's interesting! I spoke. And what are you doing in Acapulco? I asked him, he told me he was a boutique manager, then he told me that his employees had printed the T-shirts wrong, and he was upset with them. At the time, I thought, but that's what I saw when I first saw it.

I knew very well...

He told me what I was doing, I replied on vacation. He asked me if I was staying in Acapulco and if I knew where I was going to stay.

I told him I would decide when I got to Acapulco. He recommended a hotel that was close to his boutiques and was very good.

It was time to board the plane, and I sat down, in my rightful seat. His seat was further back.

As soon as the plane started, he sat down next to me, it looked like I was going to get away.

We talked the whole trip, it wasn't much, I think forty minutes.

I felt comfortable talking to him.

We arrived in Acapulco, it was quite hot at the airport, it looked like an oven, you could hear the songs of many birds that were in a cage, it looked like the decoration of the airport, very tropical.

He told me that, if I wanted, he could show me the hotel, I told him that it was perfect.

We left in a taxi. We arrived at the hotel, it looked cozy on the outside, I checked in at the front desk.

He left, but first, he asked me if I would accept an invitation to dinner that night, which would pick me up at the reception in two hours.

Of course, I agreed.

Once in my room, I showered, changed, and felt like a happy teenager.

At the appointed time I received a call from the reception, saying that there was a sefior waiting for me downstairs.

I dressed very well. As usual. He had a green Volkswagen, I went up and he took me to a beautiful restaurant, it had rock climbs, and the tables were on the mountain, very romantic, with lamps on each table. It was called El Campanario, very elegant and very large, there was a reception at the entrance, and they asked if we had reserved a table, he had already done it.

We sat, I think, at table number 25. fantastic! what an awesome place! Very romantic.

That place was great! I remember that I stopped to go to the bathroom, and I couldn't remember where the table was, I went to the reception of the restaurant, I told him that I didn't remember my table.

He asked me what the name of the reserve was and to top it off, I couldn't remember its name.!! Shame of me!!

Thank God, a waiter recognized me and led me to the table. We had a delicious dinner; the mariachis came and sang to us at the table. Unforgettable!

We had a nice evening when we had dinner. He went to the hotel and said goodbye at the reception, agreeing that he would pick me up the next day at noon, to show me Acapulco. Walking with him through the city, I suddenly remembered my dream, the one I had in Cuba, which told me that I was going to meet the love of my life at an airport, and, out of curiosity, I asked him:

---? What time did we meet at the airport in Mexico?

He told me it was about seven o'clock

I was thoughtful, but not amazed.

I spent some nice moments in Acapulco, he showed me the typical places of Acapulco, among other places we went to the port, where freshly caught fish was eaten, that typical smell of the sea, the people were very gentle, very cheerful, friendly and with the Mexican accent, very dear in my country. He had a Mexican accent too, he sounded very funny.

I had a great vacation in Acapulco. «My mom was right, she advised me to travel alone», thought because I was having a fantastic time

Two days later, he invited me to dinner at his house, told me that he wanted to prepare me a typical specialty of his.

He was a good cook, he told me.

Well, I thought about it for a moment, because it wasn't usual for me to accept, but I did. I said to myself, why not?

Somehow it inspired confidence.

I remember he made some spaghetti carbonara.

And he was right, it was delicious, it was a beautiful evening, we had red wine and for dessert I don't remember what it was.

Time flew by, chatting very pleasantly, and it was already very late, at night.

He asked me, if I wanted, I could stay overnight at his house until the next day, I was and am very conservative, I had never stayed in a house to sleep with a person I didn't know very well... I thought about it for a moment and said to myself... "Well, I'll accept, but if he tries to do something to me, I'I scream and leave."

I said yes, but I was going to sleep on the couch, and he could sleep in his bedroom.

He agreed but asked me if he could bring his mattress to sleep on the floor and keep me company. Accepted!

When I slept that night, I had a very clear premonitory dream.

which despite being by sefials I Understood the whole message.

Very well, as a story.

I remember it as clearly, as if it had been yesterday.

I was at one end of a path, as if it were a

Walkway, all along the walkway there were white bees' line up on

both sides. I could feel the sounds of the bees as if they wanted to sting. At another end of the walkway was my dad and he expected me to walk all the way

I could see, in the dream, that, I had to walk all the way alone. My dad couldn't accompany me.

He said to me from the other end:

! Be careful! they sting you.

Sting in Peru has a double meaning, it also means robbery.

I, at the same time, was very nervous to travel that long way, I was very nervous about the bees, how they moved and the roar they made, gave me like a nerve all over my body, they were all the same white and the noise. I felt something like a phobia.

When I woke up and saw him downstairs, sleeping on his mattress, I said to myself: «What?!! Am I going to marry him?!». I knew. I was going to marry him. Because the white bees were married and what they vibrated was that they were waiting for me to make a bad move to throw themselves on me.

In that dream they were predicting the future that awaited me.

It was absolutely true. I don't know how to explain it, but that was going to happen one hundred percent. I was sure.

I translated the dream, as if I were watching a story, but all the bees were him and his whole family, who would try to take my belongings.

Because I was so excited about this man, I accepted and said to myself: «Well, it doesn't matter, I'm not going to leave me! ».

And so, it happened afterwards.

After ten days of having a great time among clubs, restaurants, island rides and getting to know a little bit of Acapulco with him, the day came when I had to return to the airport in Mexico to take my plane back to Peru.

I told the whole story to my parents and brothers I was very excited, I felt in love.

He would call me on Sundays on the phone, how I waited for those calls!!

Until he decided to travel to Peru to see me and meet my whole family.

I had a rented apartment in Peru, during my vacation stay, I liked to live alone to somehow respect the schedule of my dad's house, since I liked to go out to dinner, dance, etc.

Sometimes I would arrive very late in the morning and prefer to live alone out of respect for my parents. But of course, I would visit them, and we would go out together.

The day came that his flight landed in Lima, and I waited for him very excitedly at the airport, I remember that I went with my brother and my brother-in law.

I introduced them all, I had found him a very good hotel for his stay. It wasn't that far from my apartment.

Every day we keep vigil to each other.

I showed her my bachelorette apartment. We didn't live together, but we were together all day, we went to the beach, I showed him the penas, places where folk music is played, etc.

He was very fond of Peruvian food, especially ceviche, a typical Peruvian dish, raw fish, cooked only with lemon and chili. He loved the Pisco Sour.

The moment has come for me so long: to introduce him to my parents.

I prepared a dinner party in my apartment and invited my parents to meet him.

It was very exciting, my mother, with her smiling character, made jokes and my father, more conservative, talked about everything that

Peru had to offer to foreigners, among other things he told him about Machupichu.

It was time for tea, after dinner, and he asked for my hand in marriage in front of my parents, so that they would give him their consent to marry me.

My dad joked with him and said:

"Not just the hand... Take it all with you. We were all happy, I noticed my boyfriend was nervous, but later he told me that in Sweden it wasn't like that, it was more private.

If you wanted to get married, you didn't necessarily ask for your hand in marriage, but South America is more conservative, Europe is more open.

We travelled to Cuzco, together to get to know Machupicchu.

To climb these high mountains, you must chew coca leaf so as not to feel short of breath. We were in the Plaza de Armas with the peasants. A beauty of culture, and fantastic weather, it was very cold, but sunny.

He remembered, when we had already been married for years, that, on that trip, we went to a hotel and I told the receptionist that I wanted two rooms, but there were none available at that time, so we took only one room. But when I wanted to change my clothes, I went into the closet so he wouldn't see me naked. He told me this later as an anecdote, I didn't really remember that detail, but he never forgot it, he told me that I was very extremist, although he had already seen me in a bikini when we were on the beach in Lima, but our relationship was only kissing.

It may feel very old-fashioned, but I had my own values and principles of what a serious relationship was, it was consistent with what I thought and did. For me, a serious relationship was first getting to know each other well and then, after maybe three months, having intimate relationships. In this case, it was after five months, that there were feelings on my part.

He returned to Mexico, to collect all his things, and then embarked to live permanently in Sweden, where he had all his family.

Then I also returned to Switzerland, where I lived, from there we had a lot of communication, he introduced me to his mother on the phone.

The German language with Swedish could be understood a little.

For my part, it was the first time I had heard Swedish because I spoke German in Switzerland. So, I was a little nervous when I talked to his mom, she was wondering when she was going to Sweden to meet me.

A good occasion came to travel to Sweden, a niece of my boyfriend was going to get married, there was a big party and he decided to invite me, so it was a great opportunity to meet all his family.

I thought that speaking English would have no problems for communication, since in Sweden it is the second language.

I didn't know what gift to bring for the party, so I decided to send it by mail as delicate packaging, a rose made of crystal was very sophisticated, but when I arrived in Sweden, I realized that it is a country where glass is made. So, it was nothing new.

I bought a melon silk dress in Switzerland, which was a scoop from a fashion show, and a shoulder-covering shawl made of melon silk with matching roses and matching silk shoes.

I thought that since I lived in Switzerland, I was used to attending parties, especially very elegant weddings, and I thought that I was going to be well dressed, but when I was at the party, I realized that I was too elegant, very eccentric and in Sweden it is customary to dress elegant, but very simple.

I was a little embarrassed, | looked like a rich Arab and I was like a mole in the meeting... I thought to myself, that if I had known, I would have chosen one of the ones I had at home.

I would have avoided all the stress, but you learn from everything.

When I arrived at Linkoping airport, I was picked up by my boyfriend and his daughter, in a small red Mercedes convertible, he came out to greet me and his daughter, who was fifteen years old at the time, greeted me with a red rose in her hand.

That same day he told me that his friend had lent him the Mercedes to receive me, I thought it was a nice touch.

It was very nice the way I was received, I was nervous, but at the same time happy to see him again.

The three of us went to the apartment, since his daughter lived with him, I arranged my things, he showed me everything, the apartment was small, and it was also very simple, so I didn't imagine it. I was used to living in Switzerland, I spent fifteen years living in that country, and the apartments were very luxurious.

Also, in Sweden he told me that he worked as a teacher, I thought he worked as a manager, I think we hadn't spoken very clearly about the job before.

Later, he showed me paintings that he had in his apartment, and I was very struck by a painting made of wool that was on his wall, it had Inca motifs. He told me that it was a gift that his friend gave him in Mexico, and it was from Peru, and it just so happens that it was the same year that I bought the pottery of a child in Sweden, when I was in transit traveling to Denmark. That pottery of a child who had the flag of Sweden.

It was very mysterious, things that happened parallel to both of us.

I also noticed that the houses, which had apartments as a building in Sweden, had the basement, about I had designed it in Spain, with some small windows, in conclusion, I built a house in Spain with the typical Swedish basement part. I had bought a pottery of a child's clothes in Sweden with a Swedish flag attached to it, when I was single, about five years ago and the same year he was given a painting made of Inca fabric from Peru.

Another synchronicity of fate, you might say, six months before I met him. I was in Cuba when I travelled alone. That a Cuban man in my dreams gave me instructions and told me that I was going to meet my partner at an airport at seven o'clock at night.

And so it happened, I met him at the airport in Mexico and it was at seven o'clock at night.

I've always thought about everything that happened to me, but sometimes I told it, and they didn't believe me.

And now, I decided to write a book.

Well, going back to my story, I met all her family at her cousin's wedding, all very nice, I spoke English with almost everyone, since it is the second language of Sweden, apart from Swedish, with my boyfriend I spoke Spanish, with his brother I spoke German. With his parents, my boyfriend translated for me, because they didn't speak English very well, but his sister, brother-in-law and other members of the family spoke English, without problems.

He took me to different places in Linkoping to visit, we also went to Stockholm, capital of Sweden, he showed me museums with his brother, who lived there.

We also visited the Castle of the Kings of Sweden, the Parliament, etc.

The whole trip was very interesting, his daughter was very nice, I felt that she was a little jealous of our relationship, but I could understand that, because before she had her father only for herself, but now she had to share it. I was also not so mature at that time, I was thirty-five years old, but I had never experienced a situation like this before.

NEAR DEATH ENCOUNTER

Something happened, which I will never forget when I was in Sweden with my boyfriend. One afternoon, in his apartment, I wanted to take a bath in the shower. His apartment was very small, therefore, so was his bathroom. He had a shower, the living room was next door, thank God, because if not, I wouldn't have listened.

I went in to take a shower, and I like to take a hot shower, the bathroom filled with steam, and I felt like I was short of breath, and that was the last thing I felt.

Apparently, I fell fainting to the floor, and he heard a noise suddenly, - that's what he told me.

After feeling short of breath and dizzy, I crossed the tile wall and instead of a tile wall it was an entrance with an immense yellow light that filled the entire width of the wall.

That light was nice, it didn't dazzle my eyes, I felt good, like in my house I went inside, I felt a lot of peace and security, I didn't know what was happening, I just felt that it was something natural, I wasn't afraid, I felt very, very serene, like at home.

Until, on the left side of my head, I saw a bearded senior who spoke to me in a very powerful voice, too powerful, that inspired respect. And he said to me:

«! I am Jesus! he said slowly and loudly. On the right side there was a dark-haired boy, about ten years old, he had a black jacket and light pants, I understood that he was a relative who was coming to pick me up.

The communication was telepathic, without words and I understood everything, I think he listened to the Lord, who said Jesus. But I always thought it was my brother called Jesus, when he was little, the boy who was on my right.

Then, I understood that I had lost my life and had transcended, but I asked myself at that moment, what is my brother doing here if he has not died.

know that when a person dies, the deceased family members come to receive them. And the little boy who came to pick me up alone, I didn't physically identify him, he wasn't known to me, but I was sure he was a relative.

I have had a confusion for many years, perhaps because I do not believe that the person who spoke to me was the MASTER JESUS. My mind couldn't believe it.

Since I have a brother who is two years younger, and his name is Jesus, I thought that the ten-year-old boy I saw on my right was my brother Jesus and I associated the voice of JESUS OF NAZARETH, but I thought he was my brother, maybe I couldn't believe what was happening to me with God, but I did know that I was transcending. I asked myself: «What was my brother Jesus doing there if he was alive and living in Santo Domingo at that time...? ».

I asked him if he had had a near-death encounter in 1992, he said no, but he had been very sick to his stomach.

I attributed this for many years.

I've told this to very few people. Two years ago, I suddenly started crying on a bus when I realized that it was God who had spoken to me.

I don't remember what he said to me, but it's obvious that he told me that it wasn't my time yet and I had to go back.

When I returned to the scene of the apartment, I saw myself, in the living room on my boyfriend's lap, I had my eyes open. I had passed away with my eyes open, he was slapping me and calling me by my name, my soul entered my body, but what was hardest for me was seeing with my eyes, I couldn't see even though I had them open.

They felt very hard, like glass, the pupils very hard, and finally, with a lot of effort I was able to see. I was like a fool, I had been somewhere else, I was thoughtful, I didn't tell my boyfriend anything...

«He's not going to believe me», thought. I guess I had a heart attack when I showered.

After three days I found out that I was pregnant with my first child, and that's what Master Jesus surely told me, that's why I had to go back. But I didn't really want to go back, it's something that I have no words to describe, I felt at home, with peace, as if I knew that place of my whole life and had returned, there was no fear, no negative feeling, it seemed that, being here, on Earth, we forgot our true home, where our spirit goes.

I returned to Switzerland after a week, I spent my pregnancy there until I was six months old.

We always communicated by phone and arranged for me to move to Sweden. He arranged with his dad to pick me up by car so he could take some of my things to Sweden, but when they came to pick me up, we realized that I wasn't going to be able to resist such a long car ride for my pregnancy.

They went back to Sweden on their own, and we decided that I would travel by plane before I was seven months pregnant, which is what was required to travel by plane if I could not be a risk to the baby because of the pressure of the plane.

When I was seven months pregnant, I moved to Sweden, I studied the language at school when I was pregnant, it was very entertaining, I made a lot of friends at school, I met a lot of South Americans and also from all countries, it was an international school.

Interesting, because when you arrive in Sweden, it doesn't matter what age you are, or what profession you have, you must start by studying the language.

That's how I attended my classes until I was able to cope with the pregnancy. I also remember, before I was pregnant, I travelled to Spain with my boyfriend, so that he could see my house that I had built as a maiden. He liked it very much, we had a great time getting to know Barcelona and Tarragona, where my house was located.

I showed him all the rooms, including the room where I had a child's ceramic ornament with the Swedish flag, but neither he nor I were aware of what was happening at the time even though I had had all these puzzles of my life's destiny.

Now that I am aware and can collect my whole life, I can write this book.

***

After he visited my house, I imagine that he would have discussed it with his whole family, as is normal, but that was the reason that his whole family pressured me to sell what was my house in Spain, after I married him, and they were aware of all my things as if they belonged to them. I know that in Sweden and especially when you get married, you must fight together to progress, but I didn't understand why you should share something that cost me a lot of effort alone at the time of my singleness. I separated my assets before I got married and that included my house in Spain and my bank accounts in Switzerland.

But after I got married, they were pressuring me to sell my house, which I didn't like.

There I saw my dream revealed after three days of meeting him, all those white bees were all his family, waiting for me to make a bad move to sting me. All this was reported to me in my dream, but I accepted, and said that I was not going to leave myself, because I was not stupid.

Later, when I was in Sweden, already pregnant, I realized that he was an alcoholic, and he had a lot of debts, I understand that he was the black sheep of his family and they had seen me as a solution for him to change and at the same time to pay him all his debts that he had with his parents and others stuff.

I could see this when I moved to Sweden, there was only talk of debt.

This relationship with the Swede was like a continuation of my previous partner, it was like I was continuing the story, but this time it was with a child. They were the same characteristics.

Later, over time, as I studied spirituality, I was able to understand why the same situation was repeated, but with another person. They are karmic causes, which are repeated over and over again, until one decides to accept and separate without any resentment and wishing all the good for the person.

It's the only way to avoid repeating the lesson.

I have learned that you must accept God's will, that does not mean agreeing with the person, but you must wait until that situation no longer takes away your peace. Then, we will have learned the lesson that the person came to teach us.

THEY ARE OUR MIRRORS.

In my case, the two experiences taught me that I should have SELF-LOVE.

And because of the wounds of our childhood, we don't value ourselves, we don't respect ourselves and we are very attached to people, and we project that into our adult life, when their traumas are not healed, inherited from our parents, who, at the same time, have their own unhealed wounds and did everything best they knew with the tools they had.

With these wounds we go out into the world, and we go looking for that emptiness that we haven't had since we were a child.

I have studied, through spirituality, that we are souls and that before reincarnating here on Earth we make a soul contract with other souls to come and be our mirrors, to help us evolve and remember who we are.

Spiritual beings living a human experience with this body, which is our vehicle, our ego, to be able to be in this earthly world of the third dimension.

We, on the spiritual plane, before reincarnating, choose our parents, brothers, friends and all the other people who have marked us in this life for better or worse.

Each of these souls was going to have a role, like a movie to act according to what we came to learn.

But what happens when we're born? We forget our entire contract, that's why we complain and almost always blame others, without knowing that we ourselves have designed how our earthly life is going to be, with the sole desire to evolve as spirits and, therefore, to be able to pass all the subjects we have to learn so as not to return once again to have the same experiences.

THE POWER TO DECREE EVENTS OF THE FUTURE AND VISUALIZE THEM

I'm going to go back in time. When I was single and living in Switzerland, I travelled to Peru almost once a year. On one occasion I told my father, looking up at the sky and very convinced, that when I got married, they were going to take me in a carriage with two white horses.

Curiously, after many years, I had already forgotten what I told my dad, there was a couple of neighbours in Sweden, who dressed up in tuxedos, carriages and two horses, and took us after our wedding, like a fairy tale.

There were the photographers and I greeting all the guests in a beautiful garden path full of trees on the sides, while they threw rice at me.

What a precious moment!

I invited my parents, my younger sister, and a great friend from my whole family to my wedding in Sweden.

A month before my wedding, I paid for all of them, they stayed in our apartment. We spent a few happy moments all together at home and very much fun.

When my dad saw the floats at my wedding, he was very thoughtful about what I told him years ago and he was very proud of me.

Actually, I didn't remember what I said to my dad, until I saw the float, which was a surprise to me and my husband.

Our son was born April 27, 1993.

Our marriage took place on June 19 of the same year. And the next day was the baptism of my son, who was two months old. All the guests stayed until the next day of the christening ceremony.

Then, it didn't take me long to realize, over time, that my husband was an alcoholic and his family had kept that from me. he was the black sheep of the family, and for them, I was the salvation, who was going to take care of their son, who had no responsibility and had a lot of debts in the bank.

In conclusion, he was the continuation of that other relationship that I closed. It seemed like the next chapter was coming. Same circumstances, but this time, I already had a previous experience and never left.

I had to live with him, taking care of my belongings and defensive.

My son was born, with a cesarean section, because when I was single, they removed a fibroid the size of an orange, and the doctors told me that if I had a child, it could not be born normal as all women give birth, because I could not push, it had to be under a cesarean section, and so it was.

When they injected me with anesthesia into my spine, it took almost half an hour and they finally made it, but instead of just numbing from the waist down, the anesthesia went up to my neck, and I felt like I was choking.

They put me on oxygen, and I felt better, then they took my son out with the cut they made for me. I saw his face a little purple when they put him on my chest, but when they took him out of me, they ran him away, I think, for oxygen, because he didn't cry immediately. It may have been the reason he was born with cerebral palsy.

Then everything happened, we left the hospital very happy, with our son, his physique was all normal, but my husband told me later that he noticed that he had both fists of his hands closed all the time and his feet stretched out as if he were going to dance ballet.

I had no experience as a mother, it was the first child I had and I was very happy with his presence, I played sports, I spent time with my little son, and I felt very happy.

But my husband had already had two daughters, so he already had experience.

The only thing that seemed strange to me was that he didn't sit down, I had to put pillows on his sides, and he didn't crawl when we went out

With his stroller for a walk, I would see the other children who could sit down, sometimes I would ask the mothers how old they were and since they always happened to be older than my son, it seemed to calm me down.

PREMONITORY DREAM

When my son was five months old, once I dreamed with poop, I think I was going with my son in the toilet and I found poop, it made me sick, and I went to the other toilet, and it was the same. That was clear to me when I woke up, I can't explain why, but I was translating my dreams, and I knew what was going to happen.

That dream told me that I was going to receive money through my son, and I did.

The insurance, a month later, gave me retroactive money because they had to pay me from the time, he was one month old, and this was until he turned eighteen, it was an amount that was given to the mother when she took care of a child with a disability.

After two months I had another dream with poop again, but this time it was more poop, and there was a Japanese woman in my dream who told me that I was going to gain a lot of money with my son, but It had already paid the insurance to take care of him.

That money wasn't it had to be someone else.

And sure enough, when he turned eighteen, and I was and still am his legal representative, I met a company of assistants.

It is common here in Sweden, the companies of assistants, because they give a lot of priority to special children and elderly people.

I told him about my son, I didn't have any idea about the Swedish system, I just studied the language, Swedish laws and everything that was needed to function in this society. I spoke with this company and the manager told me that he could help me request many hours as an assistant to have employees to help him in his daily life.

Amazingly, the state gave him so many hours that he could have up to seven assistants for my son, and that's a lot of money that insurance paid for me to hire a company and pick the right people for my son, without costing me anything.

That was the meaning of the second dream, but I saw that many years later.

ANOTHER PREMONITORY DREAM

By the time my son was three months old, I was already married, and I had a ring with diamonds around it that my husband bought for me. One night I went to the bathroom sink to wash my hands, I put soap on myself, and when I was going to wash, the ring that was on my ring finger slipped from my finger and fell into the hole of the sink that was in the middle. In an effort to get my ring back, I put a wire to untie and take my ring, but hairs came out instead of the ring, dirty hairs. Like when a plumber unclogs a drain.

Hairs kept coming out and suddenly a medium-sized pair of scissors came out and then more hairs kept coming out and then a bigger pair of scissors came out and then finally I took out the ring. But the ring wasn't the same, it was thicker, and the Rubies looked bigger, it was like looking at the ring with a magnifying glass, even though it was the same wedding ring.

When I woke up, I remembered the dream, and I interpreted it immediately, as always.

The dream told me that I was going to have problems in my marriage, hairs mean lawsuits and I wanted to recover my marriage at all costs, that's why I searched with the wire, but along the way I was going to have problems, messes, difficulties and the first scissors was that I was going to see a breakdown in the marriage, scissors is court, And then I would insist on saving my marriage, with lawsuits, which are hair, and then I was going to see a very big and definitive cut, that's why I saw the big scissors in my dream, and then it was going to be a very strong marriage like the ring I saw when I got it back.

ANOTHER PREMONITORY DREAM II

All these premonitory dreams were before I moved to Peru when Jonathan was six months old.

I dream of a Japanese Buddhist woman. I had already entered.

Buddhist philosophy when I was living in Switzerland as a single woman, seven months before I met my husband in Mexico.

I liked his philosophy, and I meditated every day.

NAM MIO HO REN GE KIO, which is the law of cause and effect.

I dreamed that I was in a room with men who were my students, and I was talking to them about Buddhism, I had a blackboard with a pen where I indicated to them.

I was thirty-six years old at the time I was dreaming, but in my dream, I saw myself at my age.

Currently sixty-six years old, | looked more mature and elegant, I had other fine manners, I looked pretty, an interesting woman, and I spoke very seriously, I commanded respect.

This Japanese woman told me that I was going to win a lot of rubbles, I remember perfectly the face of the lady.

When I woke up, I asked my husband which country had rubbles as currency, and he told me Russia, I didn't know before.

So far, I always wonder when I'll go to Russia, I've asked people if there are crime problems in Russia, because it seems that I gave talks to those people, and that's actually what I like to talk about spirituality. I hope that by the time this book is available to the public I will have already been giving my talks in Russia.

That is the dream that has not yet been realized, I know that everything comes at the perfect time.

MY CHILD'S ADVANCEMENT

Every month I took him to his check-up, as is normal here in Sweden, I asked the doctor why he didn't sit down, and they always told me that he would do it eventually, but as the months went by, he was already six months old, and he didn't even sit down.

That was beginning to worry me, and I was always waiting for the answer from the doctors, until he was one year old, and they decided to do an MRI in his brain.

They put him in a tunnel.

I remember my son's gaze, his frightened eyes and asking me with his eyes what that tunnel was. I calmed it down, it made me very sad, and it was the most tense and distressing day of my life, although the results were given to us in fifteen days.

I was very nervous all those days, of course, I had a suspicion, but it's not the same as being told the reality of the things, and I had a hope that my little boy would be healthy.

The day came, the doctor was going to call my husband, to tell him the answer.

My husband didn't call me, but he came home as usual, but this time with a bottle of wine, I thought it was to celebrate the good news the doctor had given him, I asked him what the doctor told you.

I was with my son in my arms, and my husband came over, the three of us hugged and started crying, my little son also cried, he didn't understand what was happening, and just then, he told me that he had cerebral palsy and had fewer neurons than a normal person, but there was rehabilitation.

After this news, I called my dad and told him in tears what the doctor told me.

My dad tried to comfort me on the phone a long time, then I called a great friend, he was in Sweden, in my marriage whom I had known since I was sixteen years old and told him in tears.

Worried, he said to me:

«What's the matter? ». Why are you crying? Your child is alive... I thought you were going to tell me he had passed away! Don't worry, everything has a solution in life, except death.

That statement stuck with me, and his words did me a lot of good.

Although I had a season that I felt very sad.

When I went for a walk with my little boy and saw other moms in their cars, I would ask myself, «why me? », and look up at the sky. I felt like a stranger in the world, different from other people.

That's how I went, I think two weeks, but then, I said ENOUGH! I made it a point to be prepared to fight for my son.

I played sports since he was born, so that my figure would go back to the way it was before. I was used to working out, running three times a week outside, rain or not, snow or no snow, three times a week no excuses, and twice a week aerobics at an academy.

Sport helped me not to think about my son's illness anymore. I was happy again in my daily life, very optimistic, I assimilated everything as if it were part of my life and I was happy all the time, I attended all his therapies with a lot of optimism.

I liked to make a lot of jokes, I enjoyed with my son in the snow in Sweden. We travelled to Spain, to my house when he turned one year old.

It was there when we were on a bus to Tarragona that we saw the first epilepsy that our little son suffered. We were amazed looking at him, how his lips turned purple, and he looked lost. Luckily, it went by very quickly, thank God.

While I attended my intensive Swedish classes, which were every day from Monday to Friday, I left my son in a Dagis. Here it gets used to it because parents go to work and leave their babies in these places, where there are many children, and very kind specialized staff.

On that side, Sweden is a very civilized and very humane country, in that place where I left my son, he was the only baby who didn't walk or crawl. He used to move around sitting crawling or upside down looking at the floor lying down like a worm.

Once, I never forget it, when I went to pick him up as usual after my school, I found him crying, a little boy who saw him move so strangely, bit his face, because he didn't understand why my son was like that.

I remember when my little son saw me, crying, looked at me, and with his eyes, he asked me: «Why? ».

Really, I asked myself the same question: «Why did that boy attack him if he didn't do anything! » was in tears, I told the staff, please take good care of him, because he didn't know how to defend himself.

My son was and is, until now, who is thirty years old, a very cheerful and sociable boy.

When he woke up, he always woke up with a smile. I've gone everywhere with him, I've never hidden him, and I've made him feel like he's a kid like any other, that's why he doesn't have any kind of complexes. He was and is the reason for my life.

I love him very much, I am very grateful to the universe, that he chose me as his mother. He likes to travel by plane very much, he has done it since he was very young traveling long hours from Europe to South America. Currently, he knows seven countries, has travelled a lot, is very polite and knows how to behave in any environment. We've usually taken trips to five-star resorts, and he's had a fantastic time.

The first time, when he travelled to Peru, he was three years old.

On this trip, it was my dad who informed me that Peru had the best hospitals for children with disabilities and neurological problems and that it would be very good for Jonathan.

Among other hospitals, there was the most famous one in Lima, with the best specialists and therapists in Peru. This hospital was state-owned, so it was very cheap, for people with very few Resources.

Generally, in Peru, the best hospitals are those of the State, since they find professionals, who really love their work, not like private places, which are very materialistic. That's what | liked. The only thing is that it was very far from where I lived, almost three hours by bus there and another three hours back.

Also, the attention was at eight o'clock in the morning. But to be the first in line, you had to go at least five o'clock and stand in line and wait for them to open, because they served a limited number of people and to be guaranteed that you would fit that quota, you had to be one of the first.

Well, going there was quite an adventure, I left home almost four in the morning. I brought him his breakfast and his bottle of vanlig that he used to take in the mornings, bananas, and other little things that he liked, he didn't walk, I carried it with me loaded and with a backpack behind me.

The first time, it was to be evaluated and given a rehabilitation plan and I was told that my son was going to walk in nine months with therapy three times a week, all his therapies, occupational, pool, physical therapy, speech therapy, etc.

Quite the opposite, before traveling to Peru, when I was told the diagnosis in Sweden. The doctors told me, that according to the statistics and as the books say about neurological diseases and the severity of the brain with less.

Neurons than a normal person has, he had damaged the left part of the brain that affected speech and the motor part.

The doctors' conclusion was that He wasn't going to walk, but in Sweden they had a lot of help with everything I needed, wheelchair, walker, etc.

With this diagnosis, I didn't stay calm, really, something in me told me, that everything was going to be solved, I was always optimistic and very happy. I even made jokes with my little son, we had a great time, he was very nice and very handsome, you can't tell him he has any problems, if he doesn't talk, he has a lot of charisma.

We were in Peru for a month and then, very excited and happy, I returned to Sweden to tell my husband about the good news.

I told him how good Peru was for our son, but I didn't see that he was very enthusiastic, on the contrary, I noticed that he was nervous to inform his mother. I told him that we had to move to Peru to rehabilitate Jonathan.

He called his mom on the phone and was telling her about Peru, and I picked up the attachment of another device, I wanted to know how happy his mom was going to receive the news of her grandson. However, instead of thinking about Jonathan, I was amazed at what she said to his son and complained to him:

«And the house of Spain? ». «You have to sell it before you leave so that you can pay off the debt! » said the lady to her son.

I was very disappointed! I thought he was interested in my son, her grandson.

Previously, during my stay in Sweden the first three Years ago, his father with other relatives, I lent them my house to go on vacation and my husband with his father told me that they were going to fix the pool, which I had, but it seems that the father advised my husband to sell my house to be able to share the profit.

I imagined that, because after having been to the house in Spain: they didn't stop pressuring me to sell it with a real estate agent, even when they came to visit us, they asked my husband in front of me, how the sale was going. At that time, I didn't speak much Swedish, I wanted to tell them so many things, but the language didn't help me, they didn't speak English.

Well, when I heard what his mother told my husband about the annex, I hung up the phone and told him that, if he didn't come, I would go alone to Peru with my son, that I had no problem.

I started selling all my furniture, at least the ones I could that had brought in a transport from Spain to Sweden, the things I couldn't sell, I put them in a container and went with Jonathan.

My husband arrived in Peru three months later, when I arrived in Lima.

In Peru I looked for an apartment to live with my son, I have always liked to be independent, and not to live with my parents, only to visit them.

Well, I lived in different places, it wasn't very easy, I was used to going to find apartments, fast for singles, but now it was with my son with a disability. It had been many years since had lived in Peru, more than twenty, only visited my family when I lived in Switzerland.

But this time life took a turn for me, returning to Peru to rehabilitate my son.

Living in Peru, where you had to fight, I didn't have the help I had in Sweden, but at that time, I didn't think about any obstacles, all that mattered to me was that my son would be rehabilitated in nine months, as the experts had promised me.

I was first in an apartment of a woman who lived in the upper part of her house and I with my son rented the first floor, I liked it, because it was located in the area where my parents lived, somehow, being close to them, I did not feel so alone with my son. But this woman made my life impossible, even though I knew that I was living with my little son who was three and a half years old.

Every time I felt like we were bathing with hot water, I turn off the water, I think to save. I paid her the entire rent in advance three months-and it was expensive, and when I mentioned it to my sister, she told me. I was not aware of the prices in Peru, it seems that the lady took advantage of it, and of course, since I paid her everything in advance, she was already cutting off the water.

I didn't have a very pleasant time there, I tried to understand this lady, but you can't change people, I just waited for the three months to pass before leaving. In that apartment, I received my husband when he arrived in Peru.

Before this apartment, I was in another one of a friend that I had unoccupied, I told her that she could rent me, and so she did, there lived alone with my son.

But this apartment was upstairs on the fourth floor and didn't have an elevator, my son had a wheelchair that I bought of the Swedish state to take it to Peru.

The Swedish state can lend a wheelchair to travel, but when the person is going to stay in another country for more than six months, you cannot bring the chair, and if you want, you have to buy it.

With his wheelchair | moved around only in taxis and vans because the buses at that time in Peru were not prepared for people with wheelchairs. So, transportation wasn't cheap at all. But I managed to bring enough money for me and my son and all the therapies I needed with my savings from Switzerland.

was always a very strong person, my mistake was that I didn't ask my family for help, I thought I was going to bother, with all the responsibility of my son, go to his therapy, think about everything, I ended up very tired at night.

Once I fainted in the apartment when I was alone with my son, I hit my head hard, I felt like I was short of breath, everything started spinning and I felt weak. I wanted to get to the couch quickly so I wouldn't hit myself, but I didn't make it, I think I was fainted for a few seconds. When I woke up, on the floor, the back of my head hurt a lot, I felt like that. Thank God nothing else happened to me, because I was alone. It was because I thought a lot and my head hurt.

As a result of this experience, I got an employee, through a friend, to work helping me and had her bedroom for her to stay over. She only had Sundays off.

In total, I was in four apartments with my son alone, the first one I arrived at was through an agency, which I used when I was single in a tourist place.; but it didn't work with my son, it was too noisy for him. I stayed there for only fifteen days.

Then my friend's apartment, which was a little small, far away and on the fourth floor, where I fainted.

And finally, I went where the woman cut off my water. In this apartment, I greeted my husband when he arrived.

I also had a piece of land, which I bought when I was twenty-six years old and it was in a place where nothing existed, it was all land.

Years later, it became a large housing estate.

I bought it, to buy something for myself, I thought that one day I would build a beautiful house, I didn't think about investment.

Something that I regret enormously, because I could have bought the entire district and today, it would be millionaires because they increased in price enormously. But there's a reason thing happen, it's clear that I wasn't emotionally prepared to invest.

The day came when my husband came from Sweden to live in Peru:

I went to pick him up at the airport with Jonathan, of course my little son was very happy, he was three and a half years old.

Then we went to the apartment of the lady, who turned off the water when I showered, but it was already paid for, the little house was very cozy, like a rustic stone house, it only had bad, the character of woman was difficult. During the period that my husband was living there with me, the lady was a little gentler, perhaps because she saw that I was no longer alone.

Meanwhile, my husband and I were looking at another rental nearby, we always asked people if they knew someone who wantet to rent.

Once we were told that a psychologist was renting the upper part of her house, in fact, she had a sign on her house outside. We rang the doorbell, and the owner came out, her name was Elena, and in the future, she became our best friend. It seems that she was very selective in choosing the tenant, very polite and friendly, she worked at a University of Psychology, she was very professional. When he saw my husband, who was a foreign, gringo, he accepted, because we were a beautiful couple, and we had a son. Generally, in Peru, at least in those years, foreigners were not seen in those neighborhoods', only in tourist sites, such as Miraflores.

He ushered us into his house, and we talked, then she showed us where the apartment was, which was completely independent and had another entrance. It was very cozy, enough for the three of us, it had a place to park the car, although at that time we didn't have it, we were thinking of buying it in the future. When we finished the contract, we moved there, very happy, above all I was no longer alone. At least I could talk to him about my concerns.

We bought, or rather, I bought the furniture needed to furnish the small apartment, it didn't take much, and we painted it. Elena was very gentle, very prudent, and soon she was like a family to us, she became quite fond of Jonathan, I always paid the rent on the right day, everything went well from the beginning.

We started thinking about finding a teaching job for my husband, which was his profession. He got very expensive private schools and was paid very well.

For my part, I began to think about what business I could have in the future in Peru, to give me time to be with my son and be able to do my sports, etc.

I showed my husband the land I had and told him we could build a very big house for the three of us.

At the same time, I began to notice that in Lima, many taxi stations were used to get around, and I thought it would be fine if I invested in buying cars and putting them to work with drivers day and night, that is, twenty four hours a day, leaving a Sunday for the car to rest. The truth is that I was not used to working with office hours, I never did it in my life, I liked to have an independent business, that could be the owner of my time and generate money at the same time.

The next step I took, I transferred my money from Switzerland to my bank in Peru, it was enough, I made an account in dollars and put it on a fixed term, at that time they paid seven percent per year, which really, with the amount I had, I could have a monthly return that paid all the expenses to live very well. At the same time, I left my house in Spain with a real estate agency to sell it, since it didn't make any sense to have a house that I almost never went to, and in which I had already been robbed three times and took things of value because the house was alone. I just hoped it would sell soon, so I wouldn't have too much to worry about.

At least it didn't come up for sale when I was in Sweden, because with what I heard from his mom who was expecting my house to be sold, I would have been very upset, I don't know what they wanted to do, but I wasn't going to let them take my money, the only way was, I think, if I divorced to divide the profits. Maybe that's what he and his family were planning.

Butt somehow, now, I realize that had someone supernatural protecting me, because have always acted innocently, without malice, and I have made timely decisions against any negative consequences.

I realized, when I showed my land to my husband, that he was very angry at me, as if to say... Everything you had and you haven't told me anything before!

I noticed this because he arrived in Peru in December, and we attended a very nice New Year's event, he had drunk a lot of alcohol and assaulted me in the street.

All the people who passed by were astonished to see a gringo mistreating a woman. I was very embarrassed, I think he punched me in the eye and I was left with my black eye.

I didn't understand why he was doing that to me. Yes, when he arrived from Sweden, after having left me alone with my son for three months, I was waiting for him in a very nice house, and everything was ready. I didn't understand why he was so angry at me!

Well, yes, then I understood. That was the first and last time I let a man beat me, because then he knew me very well.

***

In the bank where my money arrived from Switzerland to Peru, there was a promotion that, for every five hundred dollars, apart from seven percent, they gave an option for a raffle that they did once a month.

So, I had quite a few options, but, of course, it was a matter of luck, since the raffle basket was only one and all of Peru participated, with all the different territories of the country, so there were thousands of people who participated every month.

With this money, I started a taxi company, first I bought a small Tico car, it was very small. I had two drivers, but on Sundays we had the car to go around we

I made a deal with my husband, he worked in his profession as a teacher and would take care of the mechanical part to fix the car, if it broke down, I invested in buying, and I controlled the money, because every day they delivered what they worked, it was a certain amount that each driver had to give me and the rest was for them.

At the same time, I hired an architect and did all my paperwork to build a beautiful house on the land I had bought as a maiden.

The land was 980 square meters, the house built on 250 square meters, surrounded by garden, was a single story with a gabled roof, like a California house, everyone told me.

The house was built while we were renting out Elena's house. Practically, it was built in six months with intensive labour.

I waited until Jonathan was four years old, so that when he walked, I could have another child, I thought that Jonathan should have a brother, who would take care of him when I was gone. I also wanted to have the experience, of what it feels like to have a child who is born healthy, and to be able to talk to him and not feel so alone. My husband wasn't quite happy about having another child, I explained to him that Jonathan couldn't be alone in life.

I had a very different pregnancy, but I danced, I did activities at Jonathan's school, but I had a lot of nausea, and I hardly wanted to eat anything, for most of the pregnancy.

On the way to pregnancy, I became afraid. | thought that, if I was also born with a defect, I was forty years old, and there was a better chance that this would happen.

But at the same time, he said to me: «Let it be what God wants, and if you are born with a defect, love can do anything, and I surrendered to God».

Then I didn't think any more!

Throughout my pregnancy, I was in control. The neurologist was already informed about Jonathan, I told him what it was like in Sweden, that the anesthesia they gave me reached my neck and that I saw Jonathan purple when he was born, that perhaps he lacked oxygen. He was very careful at the time of the cesarean section this time, I told him to put as little anesthesia as possible on me, that I was going to endure the pain, but that it would not affect my son.

That's what he did, I even felt the scalpel cutting me until I told him, because the cut was starting to burn, they put an anesthsia in my mouth to make me sleep, to be able to continue with the operation.

Everything went very smoothly. Thanks be to my Lord Jesus.

WHEN I MADE THE TRANSFER FROM MY BANK ACCOUNT

I remember with great joy when my money arrived from Switzerland to Peru, the manager told me that there was a raffle of some gifts for all the people who had the millionaire account in dollars. I had a lot of options, since every five hundred dollars was an option, I thought and said to myself:

Oh, I have several options.

There was one jackpot and three other smaller prizes. In the previous drawing I was told that the jackpot was a late model Mercedes Benz van, but that month they had changed.

I left the bank very happy and excited; I went with my husband; I remember I told him:

«Can you imagine if we won a honeymoon trip to Santo Domingo, how fantastic that would be! ». Always remembered how nice I had with him in Acapulco when I first met him. Honestly, I missed those times, for me it was like the honeymoon we never had. I was in love and excited about him.

It was the only time I was happy in my relationship, and it didn't last long because afterwards they were filled with conflicts and problems.

Like that moment I never lived again for the next twelve years.

I imagined traveling in the Caribbean with him. I didn't know what prizes were going to be for the next month of draw.

The detail was that I took it very seriously, and asked the manager what date the draw would be next month.

The next month, I went to a bank branch near my house, they always put the names of the winners on a poster. I went there to look for my name, I was sure that I had won, it was as if I deserved it and it was my right.

When I read the list and didn't see my name, I was very, very angry and I said to myself.

To hell with this!!

And I went on with my life.

The surprise was that the next month, because I didn't even remember myself, in fact, I didn't even want to think; I was drawn and it came out on TV, they said my name and I didn't see it.

In a single basket they went around with coupons from all over Peru

In the part of Peru that participated and took out a coupon, that's when my name came out, in the midst of so many millions of names throughout Peru.

Since I didn't take interest anymore and forgot, I didn't go to the bank or watch the program.

But the bank manager, who had my sister's phone number, which I gave him as a reference, called her the next day and told her that I had won a prize, that I had to go to the bank the next day. He didn't tell her what he'd won.

My sister called me right away and told me the news, I couldn't sleep all night. The next day, before I went, I was able to call the manager to ask him what I won. I didn't do it though, I wanted it to be a surprise.

The next day we went with the bus to the bank, we didn't have a car, only the little one that we had with the drivers busy.

On the way I was very nervous, I was laughing at the nerves. And I kept asking my husband:

«What's the prize? ». Will it be a blender, a television?

It was better to think of something small.

We arrived at the bank, it was full of people in the queue, I told him I was Teresa Fageus, they told me where the manager's office was and told me to come in.

When the manager saw me, he said:

"You've won the top prize, a zero-kilometre Nissan Sentra.

I hallucinated, I didn't even have to pay taxes, it was mine!

Just as he opened the account a few weeks ago, I was negotiating with the manager to get me more interest and interest.

Joking that he might win me in the draw.

What life is like!

The manager told me:

Look, you were asking me for more interest and now you've won the car. How lucky!

I gave a shout of happiness in the office, all the people looked on and applauded happily.

Then I had to go to the address where all the new cars were and they were going to tell me what color was. It was white!

How happy I was!

They gave it to me in a month, because just on that date a famous model Claudia Schiffer had arrived in Peru, and they were not going to be able to give the awards for this model.

That month of waiting, it was eternal, I told myself and if they call me saying they made a mistake, I was afraid, until I got it.

When I told people about my experience, I told them that I knew that I had to be drawn, that it was my right and no one could take it away from me, I was one hundred percent sure, without any doubt, I don't know how to explain it.

Then I read the law of attraction, that's what I applied.

The law of attraction says that when you visualize something feeling with emotion that you already have it, that is your right, that materializes, also this same law, says you must visualize it, feel it that you already have it and not think anymore.

And that's what I did when I got upset and went on with my life,

I let it go, and it came out the next month when I didn't pay any more attention to it.

Subsequently, I was drawn four more times, incredible as it ma seem, but they were minor prizes.

The manager told me every time I went to collect my prizes that I was a witch and I laughed.

And that's how the law of attraktion Works.

The next thing I won was a state-of-the-art film camera, set of crockery, etc., and they were in short periods of about two months apart.

It had been about seven months that I had not been drawn anymore, and one day I passed by a branch of the bank that I used to go to, I decided to go in to ask how my account was, and there | met an employee of the branch of the bank where I won the car, she had changed and recognized me,

She told me:

«Why don't you send your money to this branch? ». You who are very lucky.

Finally, she convinced me and so I did.

And this was like an anecdote, the next month, a blender that I had broken down, I was going to a market near the bank to repair it and I wanted to go into the bank to make a transaction and the clerk came out and told me that she had been calling me on my phone, I told her jokingly:

«Don't tell me I've earned something? ».

«Sure», she said, it got a blender.

—¡! WHAT!! You won't believe it, but my blender just.

It had broken down and was going to repair it! We both laughed! She just told me to pass my money to that branch and I was lucky.

This event happened to me when I was twelve years old. I was a very quiet girl at home, and I didn't speak at all, because my dad was very strict and we were ten brothers, and to avoid punishment, I preferred to keep quiet and I thought a lot, my mom called me: LA CALLADITA. (THE QUIET ONE)

At school I was also very submissive and quiet when I was little, I would sit in the last seat of the class so as not to attract attention. But this changed as I grew up, I behaved very badly at school to attract attention, everything I couldn't do at home, I did at school.

I behaved very badly, on purpose, so that the teacher would call me out and take me to talk to myself in a classroom.

I liked that deep down, I felt loved, someone who caught my attention with charity and rectitude, but without violence.

So, because I liked that situation, | always behaved badly, I was even expelled from a school once.

In an elementary school. The director was very angry at me because of my behaviour. On Mother's Day they used to raffle a huge basket of groceries with many things to eat, there the mothers attended and stood in front to see if they were drawn, they raffled one basket per room.

My mom attended that day, but this time it was in the courtyard of the school.

All the mothers from all the classrooms were there, it was a giant basket that they were going to raffle.

My mother, who was there, made me feel so sorry for her, that I wished with all my heart that she would earn that basket that she needed so much.

They turned the basket around and a student took out a piece of paper without looking, but first they massaged the basket very well.

What a great surprise! My name came out, my mom won the basket!

On the other hand, the director was so angry at me that her face showed that she was not happy and said:

That's not worth it. We must get around again. I was sad, I saw my mom's face, and even though it seemed very unfair, I couldn't do anything.

So, they put my name back in the basket and moved it well. Imagine what my surprise was when my name came up again. Unbelievable!

I hugged my mom, and the director was open-mouthed.

MY STAY IN PERU FOR EIGHT YEARS

Jonathan had a therapy plan during the eight years we lived in Peru.

He was four years old at the time, we had decided that Jonathan would stay in Peru until he was twelve, and we could do his necessary rehabilitations and then return to Sweden to evolve into other more advanced things.

After attending hospitals, decided to hire a therapist to come home three times a week.

Jonathan attended two very good schools for special children. The first was a very prestigious military college and private for the quality of the staff, Jonathan advanced immensely in every way. He was there for five years. Then I put him in a state school for special children to make him more independent without much help from the staff.

He also made a lot of progress.

In the meantime, when Jonathan had about four years, I became pregnant with my second child. Jonathan could now walk.

My son's entire pregnancy, I had a great time, the only bad thing was that I was nauseous during the whole process and hardly ate.

He was also born by caesarean section, but this time, the neurologist was very careful with the anesthesia so as not to risk my baby, considering that my first child was born with cerebral palsy.

The whole pregnancy we were living in the rented apartment while our house was being built.

The house was built in six months.

So, when we moved, Emil was six months old, I think.

The house was beautiful, we were all excited, we decorated it with care.

I have always liked to have houses and decorate them; it was my passion. We buy classic and modern furniture.

We had an unforgettable party when Emil turned one year old, there My husband's daughter came to Peru for the first time to meet her new brother and over Jonathan, who I imagine had missed him.

When I settled in Peru, I began to think about the great desire I had since I was twenty-seven years old to speak to prisoners.

And so, I always told them about that great desire of my heart to the new friends I made in Peru, since my friends of school

I didn't know where they were, and I couldn't remember their addresses anymore.

When I told them about my desire, no one took it seriously, on the contrary, they joked with me, they told me to be careful, that when I went to the prisons I would stay inside and then they would have to bring me fruit on their visits, and they laughed.

Well, I laughed with them, after all, I thought they didn't understand what I felt, but I was never discouraged in my desire.

When I lived in Switzerland, I was introduced to Buddhist philosophy and when I arrived in Peru, I connected with more Buddhist members to continue in the practice.

One day, I once told a member about my desire and whether she took it seriously. The detail was, that once I attended a party at the house of one of these new friends, and I was always in the habit of commenting on my desire to people, when I talked about life, philosophizing, and on this occasion, there was a man who danced very well and was very cheerful. I asked him what he did for a living, and he told me that he was a psychologist in men's and women's prisons. Wow! I thought. And I immediately told him about the desire I had.

He asked me what I was going to talk about, and I told him that I was going to talk about life, he found it interesting, and he told me that he was going to organize a day for me to give my talks, but it was not to one person individually as I had thought, but there were many people in the room.

The day was approaching, he called me on the phone and asked me if I needed bodyguards or anything special. I told him that there was no need for bodyguards, that I just needed a blackboard and a pencil.

Months before, I had studied theatre in Lima, with a group of artists, it was a private course of three months, very interesting. I took this course, because I was often called to do television commercials and | even worked as a statist in soap operas, I thought it would be good to study theatre and this just helped me for this occasion where I had to speak for many people.

That's why I always say, sometimes you do things that at the time you don't understand why and then over time, you realize that God is preparing people for a mission.

Later, when I gave the talks, I understood that having studied theatre had helped me to move around in a scene and lose shyness in the audience.

***

The day came, I had to be very early in the morning at the address he gave me, where the prison was located. I was at home that night very nervous, I thought for a moment where to start, and I started reading books. Then I said to myself: «I don't have to read anything, everything is already in my head, and I have it in my heart, and if the time has come for me it's because I'm re ready».

All those philosophical phrases that | was collecting during my stay in Switzerland, from the little books I kept...

Selections were called, everything I had in my head was many years of reading.

Suddenly, in the evening, in front of my husband, in the kitchen, I began to cry from the emotion and joy I felt in myself heart, to be able to speak to the prisoners. That day had finally come, and I felt so grateful to God that I felt like I was dreaming.

I was happy, I was crying with happiness.

It was more than just getting a birthday present, it was something very, very big for me. Something like a boundless light. I had never really felt that kind of happiness. It filled my whole soul.

My husband saw me crying, and he didn't understand me, he told me I was crazy, of course, he didn't understand, and I understood.

I didn't sleep very well. I dressed very classic with pants, very sober, I thought I had to dress like that because it was a men's talk and I had to inspire respect for what I was going to talk to them.

I took a taxi and got there early. It was a very modest place. I waited outside in a room. I was still nervous but determined.

At that moment I saw a young man coming and sitting down, and I could tell myself from the look he was a prisoner. But something very magical happened when I saw it, apart from feeling great mercy, it automatically took away all my nerves, I felt at home, I can't explain it in words.

The time came, I went to the room where everyone was sitting, it was full, some were standing, because they couldn't reach the chairs.

There were about forty men in their thirties.

I had my blackboard and my pencil in the background, in front of me, my friend, the psychologist, was looking at me, attentive to what I was going to talk to them.

I began my dialogue by greeting and introducing myself, I told him that I was a normal human being who had lived his experiences and that I didn't want to be looked at as if I was on a pedestal speaking from above with all the comforts of money.

I told them about my life, I told them that I saw my parents fighting and I was very scared, that I had received physical punishment from my father, but before judging the parents we had to find out what their childhood was like, to realize that they did everything in their power to give us everything that they did not Had.

My parents were very poor, but we never lacked clothes or food, and I was always very grateful for that, I saw my father working hard to support his ten children.

When I was aware of all that, I promised myself that when I grew up, I was going to give my dad everything he never had and I was going to have him like a king to thank him for everything he gave me, I never thought about the blows, but about thanking.

Thanks to that feeling and that goal, God blessed me abundantly, because I was in Switzerland, and I earned a lot of money. When you are grateful to your parents, all doors open, never had financial problems and God continues to help me, giving me strength to take care of my son who was born with cerebral palsy. And I also want to help you, because I know that sometimes there are childhood wounds that don't heal, and you can take a wrong path because of the anger you have inside, that, despite having lived a hard childhood, you chose the path of goodness, which is the essence of being. And thanks to that path.

The doors of blessing were opened to me in every way, finished.

***

As a result of this talk, I was hired to go to the women's prisons with a team of psychologists, I did the work for free, because for me it was not work, it was a joy for my soul to be able to help.

Then, amazingly, I was appointed secretary of the Post-Penitentiary Board, I appeared in the magazines, and the appointment was in the Congress of the Republic. Along with other politicians.

I continued to give my contribution to society, collecting gifts for Christmas and used clothes for the children of the prisoners, because they are not to blame, they were innocent beings. I fought by explaining that, when the prisoners finished their sentences, the doors should be opened to them to get work and they could change, because if they were singled out and all job opportunities were closed to them, and I thought that it was necessary for them to be in society as good people, otherwise they could go back to making mistakes because they did not have the doors open. That by rehabilitating these people who were dangerous to society, giving self-esteem talks, we would be collaborating with society because there would be less crime.

That was my perspective. Then I had to leave the post because I had to return to Sweden in 2005.

It was an unforgettable experience, and I would like to continue giving talks to prisoners in the future.

GOING BACK TO MY EVERYDAY LIFE

My husband in Peru continued to have problems with alcohol. I bought ten taxi cars. We had twenty chauffeurs.

I was in charge of collecting and the administrative part and my husband was in charge of the mechanical part of the cars.

The problem was that he had problems with alcohol, I had to be putting him in rehab centres. That is, I had three children; my son Jonathan with cerebral palsy, my other son who was born in Peru and I was in charge of his school and my husband.

I had to take care of my things, because he borrowed from people, neighbours, etc. to drink, and I was totally focused on my son's rehabilitation, that's why I didn't get divorced. I think my son was the bond, which forced me to stay in the marriage, because I didn't have time to think about anything else.

All this made me a very strong and enterprising person, I had to do everything by myself, as a pillar of my family.

Besides, since we lived in Peru and close to my parents' house, my brothers always came to ask for help, because through all those years that I lived single in Switzerland, I had used them to help them, but then, I had a son with cerebral palsy, and it seemed that they didn't care.

For me it was really a burden to live in Peru; Eight years fighting with my son's rehabilitation, having taxi companies, seeing that my husband didn't drink, hospitalizing him, taking care of my parents, because my brothers got used to not being responsible with them because I existed and had the economic possibilities and that's how time went by...

PARANORMAL EVENTS IN PERU

But despite having fought in Peru, beautiful things also happened to me, and my wishes were fulfilled. I was able to give talks to prisoners, I studied theatre, I trained strictly three times a week, I did aerobics, dance, swimming, I worked in soap opera series, which I liked so much, and television commercials, all of that fulfilled me.

I also visited some people who lived in poverty to give them advice, and that also helped me to appreciate how | lived, like a queen, knowing that other people were not as lucky as I was, I thanked God for so many blessings.

My son was able to walk within nine months of arriving in

Peru, as they were told at the rehab center. It was a lot of interesting things, and I achieved many things in my struggle, I have nothing to complain about, everything made me learn.

There were a lot of things that happened within this time that I lived with my husband in Peru, I tried to distract myself and take things on the positive path. I had very fun experiences in Peru, I also travelled with my husband and my children to some places in the country, we went to the disco, we danced, but the last few years it was more difficult with alcohol.

On one occasion, I was at the bank doing some paperwork and I noticed that an old man came in with a cane as people who can't see use.

The sefior was wearing wrinkled but clean clothes, he was talking to a bank employee asking him something. I looked at it, but I kept doing my thing.

When he finished his paperwork, he left the bank and was heading to the track to cross. It was an avenue with a lot of traffic.

Immediately, I approached him to help him cross the track, at the same time I thought «how is it possible for this man to walk alone in these conditions, won't he have relatives to help him? How do they let him go out on his own? ».

I walked over to where he was. «I'm going to help him cross the track». «Aren't you afraid to go out alone, sir? ». Do you have relatives?

He replied that he always went out alone and found charitable people to help him. I persisted with my question and finally he told me that he had no family.

I then asked him where he wanted to go, I was going to order him a taxi and pay him to take him home.

He told me not to worry when I crossed the track with him, that he liked to walk around those places and went out once a month. «Where do you live? », I Asked

He told me that he lived in a nursing home and was run by religious nuns.

«Give me the name of the asylum and where it is so I can go visit you», I told him and added; that I couldn't that week, but that the next week I would surely go.

Before saying goodbye to him, I asked him what his name was, and he told me Felix Galvez.

Delighted, Felix, my name is Maria Teresa. His eyes were normal, he looked like he could see, but he was blind.

That month, I remember that it was October, and in that month the Lord of Miracles is celebrated, a purple month, because purple clothes are worn, it is typical for Catholics. It is customary to eat a cake that they call «nougat of doña Pepa».

I asked him if he would like to take him, and he told me whatever my wishes.

I said goodbye to him, and said:

«See you! ».

A few days later I had a Buddhist meeting, and I told a Buddhist woman that I met a man who was in a nursing home and that i was going to visit him next Sunday. I asked her if she wanted to come with me and she said:

Of course, I'm delighted!

That's how very human Buddhist people were, that's why I liked to go to meetings, it helped me a lot when I went through difficult times with my husband, with them I often went out to find other Buddhist members who had problems and to encourage them.

Such were my moments that occupied my time.

I told, I think, my parents and my husband that I met Mr. Felix.

MISTER FÉLIX GÁLVEZ

Sunday came, I met up with my Buddhist friend and we bought fruits, cookies, and things that were needed to take to the nursing home and hand out to the other elders. It was the first time I set foot on one. It was a very nice place, full of nuns, who were the staff, and quite a lot of discipline for the day of the visits. It reminded me of the boarding school for nuns that I was in my childhood, it was also for nuns, a very beautiful experience.

I asked at the reception for Mr. Félix Galvez, the blind man, I told the Mother Superior, it seems that he was the only person who did not have the vision.

They pointed out to me where his room was, and I saw an old man sitting upright outside his room, in the passageway. I approached him silently, and said from behind:

«Sefior Felix, guess who's here...».

«Mrs. Maria Teresa? ». He said with a gesture between hope and happiness that touched me very much.

I thought to myself that he was waiting for me. What would have happened if I hadn't come, what a disappointment for this Sefior.

«Yes», I said, «it's me». I came with a friend who told her about you.

He was very happy, I began to give Mr. Felix what I promised, the typical Dona Pepa nougat and other things that I thought were necessary for his daily life.

I also gave all the old men everything I had brought. We sat down to talk and the first thing I said to him was:

«Tell me, Felix, when is your birthday, to come here with the mariachis to celebrate? ».

I was amazed when he told me on May 2nd, the same day as my dad's birthday.

I also analysed that he had my dad's middle name. Still astonishing me, he began to tell me about his life, he had been a carpenter, and, in his thirties, he began to lose his sight because the ocular nerve died and there was no possibility of operation. His brothers lived elsewhere and the person who took care of him, until her last days when she died, was her aunt, who loved her very much and her name was Maria Teresa, like me, she couldn't get over my amazement. What a coincidence everything he was telling me.

I told him that my dad had the same birthday and that I was going to celebrate them both together.

Then I went to my parents and told them everything. My mom was astonished, she told me not to tell her more, because that was the devil's thing, it wasn't normal. She told me that I was always up to weird things. I laughed.

This gentleman became a great friend of mine for years, until I returned to Sweden. We went out countless times for lunch, with the permission of the nuns. I always went with my children and once, I think, my husband went to the nursing home. But I also took him to my house on weekends to stay with us, with the permission of the nuns.

I used to prepare the dishes that he liked the most at home, and once I even celebrated his birthday with my closest and most respectful friends.

Every time I visited him, I sat with him, listening to all the stories he told me about the asylum and his companions. He was very funny, a very cultured person and he entertained me a lot, I passed very nicely by his side.

Once I told my dad that I was going to introduce him to him, I organized a weekend that Mr. Felix was going to spend at my house, and I invited my dad to introduce him to this very special guy.

My dad was in the other room of my house, and I was coming to the living room to meet him, and I noticed that my dad made the sign of the cross, before I was in front of him.

I kept wondering why, but I thought my dad thought he was something from another world, I guess.

For me it was all normal and beautiful at the same time, of course there were very mysterious things, but I found it interesting and incredible, the important thing was how good I felt with this lord, I wanted to take care of him, to make sure that he was happy and that he lacked nothing. I even asked him how he could look for his brothers, who, according to him, may not have been alive anymore, because he didn't know more about them since the neighbours put him in the asylum because he was left alone in life.

I wanted to go to a TV show where they found relatives of missing people, but because of life things, it didn't happen.

On the days he came home and was with my husband, we would go to a club that we were members of. We had a great time.

I had a lot of trust with him, I told him about my husband's addiction to alcohol, he told me that he always prayed for me and my family and that one day my situation would improve.

Years went by and my dad went blind like Mr. Felix, he had glaucoma.

When they met, He already had the disease, but he could see very well.

Years later, however, he went blind.

As if that weren't enough, when my dad was eighty-two years old, he also got a disease that didn't move very well.

I had to go back to Sweden in 2005. I didn't see Mr. Felix anymore and my dad got worse. I was worried about his health from Sweden, and I tried to help as much as I could. Many times, he fell down the stairs because he couldn't see, he needed good care, but couldn't because I didn't live in Peru anymore.

When I went to visit, I saw that my younger brother had no patience with my dad and he yelled at him, it hurt me to see that situation, I also saw that he was mostly alone in his room, he had Alzheimer's as well.

As I was so worried about my father, I forgot about Mr. Felix one year, I was worried about my father because I saw that he was not attended to patiently, and I saw him sad, when I came back from vacation he said to me:

Little child... How are you...?

I tried to make him happy while I was in Peru, but when I returned to Sweden I just thought and thought, I didn't know how to make my dad well taken care of, I sent money to my brothers, but I suspected that they didn't take good care of him anyway.

I wanted to put nurses in my house to do it, and it seems that my brothers didn't like that, that I paid someone else and not them.

In conclusion, I made another decision with the help of my aunts, who looked for a private nursing home, with doctors always by hand.

I don't know if that was a good decision, but I made it, so that my dad would have company.

As is the irony of life, my father ended up like Mr. Felix, blind and in an asylum, of course, this was private, a nursing home, but the situation was the same.

Then they moved him to another nursing home near my parents' house, and there my mom and brothers visited him every Sunday or more.

My mom was very active with my dad and always visited him.

One day my dad died of cardiac arrest, just a day after the day after his birthday.

They told me that he danced a lot and was very happy.

I had a premonitory dream about two months before he died, I dreamed that somebody was taking him in a taxi to the nursing home, where he died, and my dad was singing to me (he was a good singer) Singing I'm leaving, he said.

I was shocked by that dream, maybe he already knew that when he was moved to another nursing home he was going to die. I think he was telling me to travel to say goodbye to him... [How I wish I would!

But I didn't, when I got the news in Sweden, I was very sick, almost one month without eating.

With all this that happened, I neglected Mr. Felix. I think I stopped seeing him for two years, but I had asked another Buddhist friend to visit him on Sundays. I sent her what he needed, and she, who was a very good human being, gladly did everything until the end.

When I was traveling to Peru, once I decided to visit Mr. Felix, I told him about my father's death, that's why I hadn't visited him.

I saw that Mr. Felix was very weak, it made me very sad, but from then on, I never left him again. I think he lived two more years, I used to make sure when I visited him that I would please make sure that they put his tombstone with his name on it when he died, because he paid the insurance for that. I always called him from Sweden to the asylum. The only thing that didn't occur to me was the most practical thing, to buy him a cell phone so that he could have it in his room and not have to go to the reception to talk to me, he didn't have much strength anymore and he was forced to leave the room.

It took him a while to get him there.

For a few weeks, the television would turn off and on by itself, many and repeated over and over for five days. I immediately thought that something was happening to Mr. Felix, so I called the asylum and asked how he was. They were told that he was a little sick to the stomach, and that I wouldn't be able to go and talk, but since they told me I was there, I was a little calmer.

After three days, my friend called me in the middle of the night telling me the bad news. I cried a lot at home, a lot........

The next day, I talked again with my friend about the tombstone that he ordered from me, to check if everything has been put right and at that moment, I felt a very cold, icy wind in the room, I knew that it was the spirit of my great friend Felix, who showed up to listen to what he ordered from me. I am very grateful for this experience; it was an unconditional love sure of other lives.

ANOTHER ENCOUNTER NEAR DEATH AT SEA

It was already 2005, and Jonathan was already twelve years old.

When we had just moved to Peru in 1996 for Jonathan's rehabilitation, my husband and I had agreed that we would return to Sweden when Jonathan had evolved enough with all his therapies in Peru. Especially, physical therapy, and we would have to move to Sweden again so that Jonathan could continue to evolve in other technical parts that Sweden offered.

The time came, we bought flight tickets for the four of us, us with our two children. We were arranging our bags, clothes, etc.., everything we had to carry and, of course,

Soon, my husband had a relapse of alcohol and I had to hospitalize him so that our return trip would not be ruined.

But a month before, we went to the private club where we were members, in the summer, it was very hot in that club, which was close to our house.

There we have spent very happy moments with our small children, we have camped with our tents with beds, it was very interesting for Emil and Jonathan, when we slept at night, with our little lamp. We grilled, we bathed, there were restaurants, there was everything in that club.

When we needed something, we went to the house three hundred meters from the club.

I noticed that one Sunday, when I went to the club, I started swimming in the big pool, many times back and forth without stopping, I didn't understand why, but I did it, without thinking, it seemed like was going to compete for a swimming Olympics. In that year, I was forty-eight years old, I was very sporty and I still am.

I swam and swam, I think twenty or twenty-five times without stopping, back and forth, I didn't know why. My husband asked me why I swam so much, it was a rare thing for him, because I had never done it.

I told him I didn't know, and I kept going, I didn't stop even to converse.

A week later, had to admit him again, because he relapsed, and we already had a date to fly back to Sweden.

When I was alone at home, once, I remember it was Saturday and I had an unexpected meeting with friends. We had a drink and the next day I was hungover.

Previously, I had organized and planned with another friend and with her son and mine to go to the beach on Sunday, but by chance that day I was with the hangover of Saturday, although I still fulfilled what I planned.

I thought I wouldn't be able to drive because I'd had a drink the night before, that I wouldn't be focused to do it, and I went to get my brother to drive my car and take us to the southern beaches. He told me he couldn't, I stopped by another friend's house and didn't find him.

So, I decided to drive myself.

It was an hour's drive on the highway, I concentrated very well, knowing that all the people in my car were under my responsibility.

Finally, I arrived very well at the beach, we parked. The beaches in the south were cleaner, some beaches were dangerous.

When I got to the beach, I saw a yellow sign, which said that you should be careful because of the current, and they put in a part «danger zone», since there were some black rocks in that area.

We stood away from that sign, but I didn't take it too seriously. account.

I started diving under the waves with my friend's son, who was fifteen years old, over and over again, I was so funny.

My seven-year-old son and twelve-year-old son played in the sand making holes, as they used to. While my friend was sunbathing with them, I dived under the waves, had a lot of fun with Israel--that was my friend's son's name- and we stayed like that for a long time, until I threw myself down once more, but this time when I stuck my head out, I was well away from my friend's son.

It was as if I had skates on my feet, which I wore without feeling.

I saw my children very small in the sand, it was very, very far away, the current had taken me towards some very large black rocks.

I yelled at my friend's son by name, and he noticed, he knew how to swim very well, I went up and down with the waves to keep me floating.

My seven-year-old son tells me that he saw only my head going up and down and my arms that I moved to keep me up.

When my friend's son saw me, he started swimming to meet me, when he was a little close to me, the current carried the two of us even further in.

He couldn't get very close to me, because I was around a whirlpool, to this day I remember the noise of that circle,

It was like a monster.

He threw a fist at my back and told me to move my feet, because if I wasn't going to sink, no one would have been able to rescue me, I was impressed.

Then, I remember that I moved my feet with such force that with my toenails I tore Israel's back.

I told him not to come close, to leave, I didn't want anything bad to happen to him to save me, I didn't want him to die. I kept screaming for him not to worry about me, to go away and save himself.

I knew that if I held on to him, I was going to panic, and that's when, sure I was going to drown. I came to think there was no way out.

At that moment I said to myself: «Death took me by surprise! ».

I felt a little angry and continued talking to myself:

«Why didn't they warn me? », I felt that something was wrong with me and that was the day I had to die.

I remember looking up at the sky with inexplicable peace and acceptance. For a few seconds I forgot that I was in the sea. I looked up at the sky and felt at home, welcome, I had no fear, just acceptance.

But then, I had a telepathy with God, I looked at my children, they looked like little ants, and they were going to be left alone so small.

My husband was in rehab and my kids were going to stay for the adventure.

My son Jonathan was digging holes in the sand, but at the same time looking thoughtfully at the sea and Emil was standing.

It seems that God asked me telepathically if I wanted to go on living and my answer was yes, for my children.!

There was telepathic communication with Jesus of Nazareth. At that moment, my seven-year-old son alerted the beach guards, but they hadn't noticed me, nor the people on the beach.

I'm sure God used my little boy to warn the lifeguards.

Immediately, two men jumped in with an orange fisherman's rope, it was far away.

My friend's son told them to both take care of her, that he could swim.

They couldn't get close because I was in a whirlpool, they yelled at me to grab the rope and luckily, I did it at the first throw. They were swimming a hundred meters ahead of me to pull me like a crane. I took the rope as if it were my life, that's when I really realized that it was coming out. The lifeguards shouted to me from afar when a wave was about to come, to take a breath and hold my breath, the wave was spinning me, I saw bubbles, I was spinning with the wave, I held my breath and wouldn't let go of the rope, I was spinning in the sea, I wanted to live.

Then I passed another wave, I did what they shouted at me, we were almost on the shore.

When I got to the shore, I thought I was already dead, that I was already in the afterlife, I arrived without my bikini top, I felt very dizzy, as if I had drunk beer.

The people standing looking at everything, they started applauding because they saved a life, I didn't faint, I didn't drink a drop of water, it was truly incredible the physical strength I had.

They interviewed me, asked me if they had to take me to the hospital for a check-up, I told them I felt fine, I was in shock.

They asked me how old I was, I said forty-eight years old. They were amazed because I had a lot of stamina for my age, they also told me that, if they rescued me three minutes later, I would have sunk, and no one would have been able to do anything.

They also told me that what they feared was that the waves, when the crashed, would drag me to the rocks and make me feel like a crash smashed my head..

I hugged my kids tight and drove back home. On the way, I made a joke to them:

«Who would have driven if I had drowned? ». That's when I understood why I was training to swim a week before at the club, it was to prepare for this event.

This was the hardest thing I ever experienced, because in other encounters to death that I had, in the Amazon, I was almost going to drown, but it was quick when the dwarf saved me.

Also, when I transcended in Sweden, while I was bathing, I went into cardiac arrest, but I didn't feel anything, only dizziness and shortness of breath, there my soul went through the wall, and I saw a yellow light.

But at sea, it was the most terrifying experience I've had so far. After this happened to me, I wanted to be alone in nature, I don't know why, but I needed to be alone with myself.

Every time I told this experience, I always cried, then it got better until I tell it now and I don't have much emotion.

But today something different happened to me, eighteen years have passed.

This was in 2005 and now we are 2023.

At this moment that I am writing this book here in the library, that emotion came back again, and I began to cry with a lot of feeling, I told it to the lady who works here. Returned that feeling.

The day after the accident, I got out of bed as if I had been.

A truck would have run over me, my whole body hurt, all my bones, I think it was the crashes of the waves.

I called my husband to the rehab centre the next day and told him that I was miraculously alive, he was amazed.

The day of our trip arrived, we were carrying a lot of things, we left all the furniture of the house in one room and left, my dog was left in charge with a friend, I regret so much not having brought him with me, because he was another son, but at that time I did not understand.

We arrived in Sweden in 2005, my husband asked me for a divorce a few months later, I really felt very grateful that we separated, because I wasn't going to live that environment of alcohol, it was very traumatizing.

He lived alone and so did I with my children, who visited him every two weeks. He continued to work as a teacher, but he continued to drink on the weekends.

***

That same year, I met a Swede, nine years younger than me, but it wasn't noticeable, since I've never looked the age I am.

We were together for almost five years, but I really think the first three were happy, I didn't want to live with a man again because I came from a bad experience, I preferred to live as lovers.

He asked to have a child with me a few months after meeting me, I think because of my age, it was the limit, he didn't have children and he sure wanted to have one with me. I told him no, that I had my children, and I wasn't going to start again, and above all that.

I had a special son, who had my full attention. He got along very well with Jonathan, he had a lot of patience, but with Emil I think he was jealous, and Emil was jealous of him too.

My kids had never seen me in any other relationship than their dad. I was very much in love, that was what I was missing, because I hadn't really had that feeling with my husband for many years.

I lived and enjoyed this experience, for the first time that the chain of meeting alcoholic partners was broken. He was quite the opposite, well-working and organized, which I wasn't at the time, since I was only studying. I think I met him at one time, which wasn't the right one.

Well, over time I realized that he was getting bored, he wanted to start a family and with me he was already losing his years, and he wasn't so young anymore.

Deep down I knew that this relationship was going to end, but I continued. In the end, I became so attached to him, that I suffered quite a bit when it was all over.

Just in 2009, my dad's death, he ended up with me, my mom was in serious condition after my dad passed away, she was sick from rife, from suffering from high blood pressure all her life, and when my dad died, my mom was very depressed and didn't want to live anymore. I cried when I was alone looking at Dad's picture.

When I broke up with him, they cut off all the friendships we had in common, they didn't want to stay with me anymore, even with my best friend and another friend that I trusted quite a lot and we met often with my boyfriend. She betrayed me, behind my back. I was planning to take my crush away from me and he was to stay with her sister.

Well, I went through all those disappointments together, thank God I was with my children, because I felt very sad.

Later, over the years, I understood that there is no evil that does not come for good, and that God closes doors to open better ones.

I became a very responsible and independent person, all the qualities I liked in my boyfriend, I got when I was alone.

Parallel to this relationship, my ex-husband had a relationship with a Swedish teacher who taught at the same school as him.

I saw my ex-husband very well in this relationship. We still had a few moments of falling in love with our respective partners, and a lot of coincidence that we both ended our relationship almost at the same time, things of life.

From then on, he never had another partner, and neither did I.

We were good friends separately me and my husband, sometimes we argued over the children, but in general, I lived my life very independent and strong, above all.

I dedicated myself to studying Swedish again, because | hadn't spoken it for eight years, I studied Swedish law and all the courses that were required. I also later studied marketing, but I couldn't work on that because my son required a lot of attention, plus I didn't sleep well at night, because I had to sleep with him.

Then, he began to have very strong epilepsies.

Sometimes I would ask myself why I studied so much, and I would say to myself, «Someday I'll understand».

And sure enough, when my son turned eighteen, he needed a legal representative, that's the law here in Sweden. And thanks to everything I studied, I was able to be their representative, otherwise the government would have chosen a Swedish citizen to represent them and that, for me, would have been very difficult. Because his mother didn't count much anymore, but his representative was the one who decided for him.

That is, I would not have been able to travel with my son anywhere without asking permission from his representative and waiting for his response. I thank God for helping me, and just intime I ended the relationship with the Swede, I was distracted and would not have been able to represent my son.

Everything is just and perfect what God does for us.

It's all for the best.

When I started looking for a job in my profession, I told them about my situation that I didn't sleep well at night because of my son, they told me that I wouldn't be able to work that way, they advised me to do paperwork so that my son would have assistants and I could have a quiet life and work, but that way they couldn't give me work.

They gave me a phone number of an assistant company, I contacted them, and the manager of the company in a period of four months, was able to do all the paperwork with the insurance and managed to get them to give him 560 hours per month. That meant twenty-four hours a day as an assistant, the maximum that insurance provides, depending on the needs of the special child.

All this paperwork and the search that I did would not have been possible if I hadn't been my son's legal representative.

Here was the premonitory dream that I had when my son was six months old, that I realized that my son was in a toilet of a lot of poops and a Japanese woman told me that with my son I was going to have a lot of money, this was what they were referring to, once again, my dreams come true.

One of his assistants is me and I organize how other attendees have to treat him, which I choose myself, and they are all Spanish-speaking, South American.

Because I am my son's legal representative, I do my best to raise funds for different therapies that my son needs, and I do everything in my power for my children's well-being.

My ex-husband unfortunately continued with alcohol here in Sweden as well, he had been working as a teacher since 2005.

When he ended the relationship with his partner, I think he went back more into alcohol. I knew that working as a teacher for him was what kept him in a discipline so that he didn't drink so much, but something inside me told me that, when he retired, he would drink without limits because he would have no obligations.

Of course, when he worked, he took the weekends, he had closed in on himself, sometimes my children went to see him and he didn't open the door of his house, even though he was inside.

He behaved in a very strange way; he didn't want to see anyone.

My son had to stay away from him because it was psychologically damaging his spirit. It was very negative, and my other special son for many years, He didn't want to see him anymore.

The father of my children passed away in December 2021 at his home; alone, from cardiac arrest. He was found after days on the kitchen floor of his home.

Once his daughter knocked on his door, and seeing that he did not answer, he sent the police to open the door and they found him on the floor, on the table there were some pills for the headache.

I'm very sad that I couldn't help him. When I had a heart attack in his Singel house, he was there with me and I was able to recover, but that's life; The soul of each person knows the day and hour that will transcend.

It was a big blow for my youngest son, my eldest son, who has a disability, I didn't know how to say something so serious, even though he hadn't seen him for years, He used to talk to him on the phone, but since you don't understand him when he talks on the phone because you can't see his expression and the signs he makes with his hands, You can't understand him at all, because he doesn't pronounce any words correctly. I didn't know how to tell him, but it seems that he understood it little by little, he never asked for him again, he seemed to understand that he was not here on earth.

On the third day after his death, he appeared to my son to say goodbye, because I saw my son's expression, he was crying a lot with a lot of feeling and he was looking up, something truly inexplicable.

Special children are pure souls, who incarnate on earth to teach human beings what kindness, patience, tolerance and unconditional love are.

I accompanied my youngest son in his grief, he felt a little guilty because he didn't see his father much, and he moved away from him, so as not to be affected by his pessimistic way of being and made my son feel guilty.

But he tried to visit him many times, knocking on his door and he would open it, so it happened on many occasions, and he made his decision for his peace of mind that it would not be affected.

For reasons of life, my son became interested in spirituality a year before this event, he wanted to look for answers to why his father behaved this way and he became very spiritual.

I think this has been the foundation to be able to live through something as hard, as is the death of his father. He was preparing himself with spirituality, he knew deep down that his father was going to end like this, he was on the way, and my son's frustration was that his father did not let himself be helped, on the contrary, he isolated himself from the people who loved him, and the same thing happened with his Swedish family, his daughter, brothers, etc...

I tried to explain to my son that everything he did for his father was what was in his hands, that everything was fine, that there was no blame, only learning.

The death of my ex-husband made a great awakening in me and my son. With him I discovered that death does not exist.

***

When he passed away we went to his apartment and saw everything he had left before he passed away, we saw the bread he had eaten in the living room, together with his glasses, which I imagine he was looking at his mobile phone or reading the newspaper. In the bathroom, there was his blue dressing gown, as if he had gone somewhere, in the kitchen, where it was the place that gave him the heart attack and fell on the floor, there were some paracetamol pills for the headache.

My son Emil said:

«It can't be that a person disappears like that, he must be somewhere. He shouted, "Dad, Dad, where are you? ».

Now as I write these lines, tears fall into my eyes, remembering my son's expression of bewilderment and sadness, but also with the conviction that he must be somewhere not visible.

Through Facebook and online media, we found a medium, who, for reasons of life, caught my attention.

A month before the death of the father of my children, I told my son about this person, the opinion she had of transcendence corroborated what I had been hearing lately in the media of YouTube, and I had also experienced a near death encounter, when I suffered a heart attack and came to light.

I decided to connect with this medium via wasap and made an appointment to communicate with my parents.

The day came, I was very nervous, I had never done that kind of session.

Actually, I gave her the name of my parents a day before our meeting by video call, and sure enough, my parents arrived, she described them as they were, but they were healthy and younger.

He communicated things to me that only my parents and me could know. They gave me a lot of advice, but it left me very happy, because they were both together.

My mom passed away with a lot of pain, I told her it hurt me.

A lot of seeing her, but she told me that she felt pain at the beginning, but at the end, she didn't feel any pain, even though she was still with us, I think the soul detaches itself before passing away to prepare to transcend.

When we went to the funeral and there was the coffin that had the body of the father of my children, despite seeing that everyone was crying in immense pain, I was happy for him, because now he was with his parents and he would no longer feel alone or guilty about anything, that is what I thought to myself.

But I was very sorry seeing Emil's sadness, I didn't take my son Jonathan, because he has cerebral palsy and is very sensitive, I don't know how he would have taken that moment so sad.

A few weeks after his death, we decided to contact the Peruvian medium; I was very sure that he had gone to the light, that's what I thought because of the experience | had when I had a heart attack... But I was surprised, the medium told me when she tried to connect with him, that he was in a dark room, she told me exactly how he used to sit, and that's how she saw him, he told her that his head hurt a lot, that's why I saw the pills in the kitchen of his house that he took, before the heart attack. He pointed to the medium his glasses and that was so that we would recognize that it was him.

Again, we attribute the lenses we found on his little table in his living room when we arrived at the apartment after he passed away.

I mean, he was the same as he used to be in his apartment, maybe he didn't know that he had died, thinking and thinking, feeling guilty about his whole life that's why.

He didn't go towards the light. That's why he drank alcohol. There he was, he didn't want to listen to the medium, it was the same situation he was in here on earth, he just changed plane. It gave me a lot of grief and concern.

The medium advised us to light a candle for him for a month and every day to talk to him with a lot of love. And that's what we did every day, I told him about all the beautiful things we had experienced in Acapulco, that he was a good person, that he didn't feel guilty about anything, that he did everything he knew and could, that only on the other side is the light, that he should go there so that he could find his parents, that no one there is going to judge him, and he wasn't going to have any more headaches. Every day it was me and my son.

After twenty days, we could no longer resist knowing how he was doing, and we made an appointment with the medium.

He was in a wonderful place, with such bright colours, lots of vegetation and a lake, he was with a relative, I think it was his grandmother, but young, the medium described her with the old clothes that were used here in Sweden.

He was amazed by the place, very happy, thanking us for helping him transcend into the light, upon awakening.

He also said that we had talked to him too much, that it was very intense. He made us laugh a lot when he made that comment, the medium also told us that he didn't speak Spanish well and had a strange accent, we knew that.

There I understood that the man I saw at the airport for the first time, with such a great light, was a great teacher who was going to take me to the spiritual world and discover that death does not exist.

That our soul transcends to another plane, which is not the earth, to continue evolving as the spirits that we are, that the body is only a means that the soul must have to experience all the experiences and lessons that we come to learn in this short period of life.

A look inside me that made me wonder who I am,? Why I am in this early life ?

My whole life has been a struggle and learning through experiences.

But something marked me and made me hit rock bottom, it was the beginning of the path to spirituality, from there I can deduce, that everything what happens is perfect and everything come in life when you are ready to understand it.

I analysed in my live that I had several unhealed childhood wounds, to know them, I had to change my misunderstood belief system.

In that year, COVID 19 time came. A brother of mine who lived in Peru was taken to the emergency room, he was short of breath and was intubated, he was very sick, he had an experience close to death.

Of course, I immediately helped him with the clinics and everything that was necessary to save him, that he was in my hands.

Actually, throughout my life I helped my whole family, I felt that since I was so blessed by God, I should help everyone, because they were less lucky.

At the same time, I analysed that I was very controlling, I wanted to have everything under control, so that they wouldn't abuse me, at the same time.

I was very distrustful of people.

I realized when I hit rock bottom that I had a big wound from childhood abandonment.

It happened that my brother recovered a lot, he continued to do his physical therapies, but he had already come out of the gravity, then since I no longer sent large sums because he did not need more care, he told me once that the doctor had diagnosed him with an incurable disease and that he practically did not have much time left. I was worried, and at the same time I had the intuition that he was lying to me. I told him to give me the doctor's number, I noticed that he hesitated to give it to me, but finally he gave it to me.

This made me even more suspicious.

When I wrote to the doctor, he confirmed what I intuited, that he was fine, and only needed therapies and with time he would get better, and he did not have a serious illness at all.

This hurt me so much, so much, because I thought, if I have given everything for him... How is it possible that he wants to emotionally blackmail me so that I keep giving him more money?

I had already gone through a lot of fear and fear, nervousness because of how serious it was, and when I was already recovering, he told me this big lie!

I felt so bad, I felt like I was garbage, with so little self-esteem and I made a compilation of my whole life for the first time. Always helping and helping, no matter how much I gave, my effort, my money, my energy and it was never enough!

I asked myself, «Who am I? Why do I exist? I deserve to be happy!

It couldn't be possible that all my life I had helped the whole family, and they didn't value me.

I fell into a very big depression. Because on top of that, I noticed that I was worried too much. I couldn't sleep when something happened to my brothers, I helped them immediately with any amount of money, I thought it was up to me whether they lived or died because I was the one who had been lucky, and they hadn't.

That's how I thought, sometimes I even forgot to take care of my son with a disability to help them, I worried too much, however, my other brothers were not affected as much as I was.

After this disappointing experience, it was the first time I asked myself, «Why do I suffer like this? ». It has nothing to do with them, it has to do with me. Why do I feel this? What takes away my peace?

I decided to make an appointment with a psychologist, and I told her how my childhood was, she helped me more than anything to let off steam and cry, for the first time in my life I told my childhood to a stranger, and I could cry.

I had four sessions with her. Then I realized, and so did she, that I didn't need any more appointments.

What really helped me understand it all was spirituality.

I decided to block out all my family and all the friends who knew my family so that I could have peace of mind and be able to be with myself.

It was the first time in my life that I wanted to get to know myself, I had never had time to do so because I was prioritizing the needs of others.

First time, that I was in first place in my life.

I bought self-help books and started watching videos on YouTube, about self-esteem.

Now I can understand why he helped in a way that wasn't normal, always wanting to help. It was because of the childhood wounds I had and I wanted to fill that void by helping my brothers to value me and love me, something I didn't perceive at all, because there were many of us.

But what I understand now... Who's going to respect me or value me if I don't do it to myself? Nothing and no one outside can give me what I need.

Love begins with oneself.

From there we are going to vibrate in that energy, and we will attract people who love us.

I realized that my brothers were my mirrors, they didn't respect me because I didn't respect myself.

It is the Law of the Universe.

You attract what you are.

I also realized that all the help and control I was exerting was because I expected something. It wasn't a healthy love; it wasn't giving without waiting.

I wanted to fill that void.

When I understood all this, after six months I connected again with my family, but not from victimhood, nor blaming them for my discomfort, but understanding that the power is within me, and if I want to do something from the heart without expecting anything in return, I do it; But if I don't want to do it, that's okay.

Don't feel guilty, it's better to please yourself than others.

That I don't need anyone to value me, I do it myself. I don't need anyone to respect me, I do it myself, and when I look in the mirror, I love what see.

Everything outside can't influence you, when you know who you are.

At the same time, with spirituality I learned that we are all evolving souls, and planet earth is a school of souls. We're all mixed.

I learned that when I helped my brothers and sisters, and didn't let them learn for themselves, I did them a disservice and they didn't evolve.

I learned that each soul comes with a plan designed to learn the lesson that corresponds to them, and it is against the law of the Universe to intervene in their learning path.

I learned that you could help with wisdom, and to help a person you can't sink into the mud with them because then we both sink, you don't have to be emotionally involved to help, instead you can give them support all the way to encourage them to follow their plan. that in the end it's all for our spiritual growth learned that if you don't love yourself, you enter into toxic dependent relationships,

It is very important to heal their wounds so as not to suffer and not blame the external.

Now I have a more respectful relationship with my brothers where they tried again to ask for financial help and I was able to be assertive and say no when I feel it, without feeling guilty.

I gave them help a few times, but it was my will, without feeling obligated, or expecting anything in return.

I've learned a lot of things with spirituality, it's a new awakening for me and I'm still learning, because while we're alive we learn all the time.

We are powerful beings, and we create our destiny in every present moment with our thoughts.

The universe does not differentiate between good and bad. The universe is an echo of our thoughts and emotions, so it's best to use thoughts to our advantage.

THE END

AUTHOR'S NOTE

I write this book to make people aware of the importance of forgiving their parents and being grateful to

them.

God blesses children who thank their parents, from there began all the blessings for me and good luck. Abundance follows me in every way, it all started with my heartfelt gratitude to my parents.

I would change absolutely nothing from the past, thanks to everything that happened in life, it made me stronger, and I became the person I am today, and I am immensely grateful to my parents for giving me life and having learned the lessons I had to learn, and I continue to learn after the death of my ex-husband.

We are unique and unrepeatable beings, we are all light and each person shines with their own light. We don't have to compare ourselves to anyone, the only person you have to compare yourself to is the person you were yesterday.

It's important not to forget where you're coming from, but it's also important to know where you're going.

THANKS

The first people I have to name are my parents, I want to honour them with my story and I thank them immensely for agreeing to be my parents.

With them I learned and continue to learn everything that my soul shows me in this great school of life that is called Earth.

To my son Jonathan because thanks to him, I understood what unconditional love is. With him | learned to bring out the best version of myself, he gave me the weapons to draw strength from within me and fight with any obstacle to achieve my goals.

To my son Emil who, at only seven years old, was the first person who realized that something was happening to me at sea and alerted the lifeguards. Thanks to him, such a mature and spiritual being, at his young age we can talk about any subject. I have a great friend.

Made in the USA
Middletown, DE
01 April 2024

52249060R00080